SURVIVING THE TEENAGE HEART ATTACK

The Heart-stopping, Jaw-droppin' Real-life Stories That Uncover How To Jumpstart Any Difficult Conversation, Crush Your Relationships And Get A Pulse On Your Purpose In Life

PATRICK NASH

DEDICATION

To all the teens that have greatly impacted my life and encouraged me to write this book.

To my wife, Tara, who sacrificed hours and hours of awesomeness with me in order to get this book written and published.

To my parents, Bill and Kathleen, who always believe in me no matter what crazy endeavor I take on.

CONTENTS

PART THREE:
RELATIONSHIPS

INTRODUCTION

L et's get straight to the heart of the matter. Being a teenager is rough. In this crazy and fast-paced world of smartphones and social media, the stress and anxiety you face every day is off the charts. You're struggling with obstacles no generation has ever had to deal with before, and that's on top of the ones young adults have dealt with since the beginning of time.

Before we begin to unpack, why don't you step into my office, and we'll run a few diagnostics? Let me know if any of this sounds familiar.

Tough times communicating with your parents? Maybe you feel like they don't always understand where you are coming from? Check.

How are things with your friends? Peers at school driving you insane? Alright, we'll check that off the list as well.

What's that? You're dealing with heartache? Maybe your crush barely knows you're alive, or you're in a relationship and having trouble navigating some tricky waters? Okay, we'll check that box, too.

Let me ask you one more question: Is there a constant yearning deep down in your heart of hearts to find what you're living for? Yeah I had a feeling that might be the case.

Okay, so let's sum up those symptoms, shall we? You want to avoid difficult conversations, you're trying to find your own set of keys to your relationships, and that search for purpose is eating you up from the inside.

I think I know the problem here, and I have a diagnosis. Your symptoms are serious, and they seem to be consistent with that of being a teenager.

Once upon a time, I was just like you. As a young adult, I hit the highest of highs and lowest of lows. I found love and was shattered by heartbreak. I was a nerd and a jock all at the same time. My parents were together and my parents were apart. I smiled on the outside to hide what I felt on the inside. I did the unthinkable: I survived being a teen.

How did I do it? After thousands of difficult conversations, multiple relationships, and hundreds of purpose-seeking missiles fired throughout my life, I discovered the answers through experience, research, and most importantly, from teenagers like you. For the last twenty years, I've either *been* a teenager or I have worked with them. As your driving instructor, I trusted you to take *my* life into *your* hands while we talked for two hours about whatever you wanted (Thank you, by the way, for giving me a mini heart attack when you swerved and missed that telephone pole by inches). As your teacher, I have experience with just about every one of you, whether you were kicked out of public schools (some of the most loyal students I ever had) or an honors student acing physics and stressing about Ivy League admissions. In my time as a teacher I've connected with the wind ensemble enthusiast and the creative artist who drew some sweet pictures on my math tests. I have successfully coached you athletes out there: from those with the hottest tempers throwing over the water cooler to the meek athlete that literally never said more than one word to anyone. As an assistant principal, I continue to kick some serious behind (figuratively) with helping 'troubled students'—as some may call you—find success in your niche. My life literally revolves around yours.

On my last day as a teacher, before I took on my current role as assistant principal, I designed a lesson on life. I taught my students not only how to navigate their teenage years but how to get out of them alive and thriving. To say my class reacted well would be an understatement:

> "Mr. Nash just taught us more about life in 45 minutes than we learned in four years!"
>
> —Vanessa L., Witness to the Last Lesson

> "You gave me the chills. Everyone should know your story. You should do this for a living!"
>
> —Michael W., Witness to the Last Lesson

I 100% believe in you having a positive impact on this world, and I want you to have the tools for success in areas where I struggled. I want you to be equipped to handle your relationships with the various lucky people you interact with throughout your life. I want you to find peace, happiness, and guidance toward fulfilling your purpose. Using my real-life experiences—which I maintain to this day could have been a hit drama series—and the CPR method I created, you will be able to tackle any difficult conversation, navigate through the ins and outs of relationships, and zone in on why you're here on this crazy, beautiful planet called Earth.

PART ONE

HOW TO ROCK A DIFFICULT CONVERSATION

CHAPTER 1

THE ANIMAL INSIDE YOU!

Before we can move ahead and get into the heart and flesh of where we're going, we need to first acknowledge where you're at. As teens, you are currently in the midst of one of the most difficult, unpredictable, and insane times of your life. One day you feel like you are on Cloud Nine and the next day you are in the deep, dark cellar of the dumps. Your life schedule is so jam-packed with school, homework, sports, theater, band, gymnastics, work, volunteering, studying, etc. that you find yourself barely able to come up for air. Or maybe you're the opposite; maybe you feel as though you are absolutely bored out of your skull and find that nothing you do feels rewarding. No matter what your life is like, I know it's probably not an easy one.

I think there's really only one way to describe your life and that's through the animal kingdom. If there was one animal in the world you could choose to describe you at this moment, what would it be?

No seriously, stop reading right now and think about it.

Okay, you got it?

Perfect. I know what you're thinking. You, my friend, are a DUCK.

Alright, I know you were probably thinking of yourself as something much more exotic, like a tiger or a unicorn. But hear me out for a second here. Picture a duck on the water. On the surface, it appears to be effortlessly gliding on the water, but underneath, its legs are paddling like crazy. In the air, a duck might be flapping its wings to stay up or soaring smoothly mid-flight, when out of nowhere, someone takes a shot at it, and suddenly, that duck is fighting for its life, dodging bullets at every turn. Or how about the chaotic aftermath that comes when a duck gets a little too close to another duck's nest. Certain people "driving your quackers"? Any of this sound familiar? I'm calling it. Looks like a duck. Talks like a duck. Waddles like a duck. Like I said before, during your teenage years, you are a duck.

But don't worry; not all ducks are created equal, and I want you to narrow it down a little bit further. Pick out what type of duck you are from the list below:

Daffy Duck – A little wacky but clever. You may have a tendency to get a little jealous, and may like to stroke the old ego at times.

Drake – The name of a male duck but more well-known as one of the flyest rappers and recording artists ever. You have a way with words, creativity, and style, and you want to be in the spotlight.

The Duck Hunter – You have a sweet beard, love the outdoors, and could give a duck what everyone else thinks about you.

Rubber Ducky – You're just trying to stay afloat amidst the commotion, but feel like you're constantly getting pushed under by external forces, a.k.a an older sibling, the neighborhood bully, the crazed teammate, etc.

Sitting Duck – You spend a lot of time sitting on those tail feathers achieving greatness when it comes to COD or Fortnite, until you get blasted by your parents or teachers.

Duck, Duck, Goose – As one of the two ducks, you sit patiently and politely waiting for greatness to happen, but for whatever reason, no one notices you, only that darn goose...

Head of the V – You like to be the leader and improve the lives of others. You know how to stay the course and love to spread your wings and fly.

The Mighty Ducks – You're the underdog (or underduck), but that doesn't stop you. You feel like no one gives you a chance and you have to continue to try and prove yourself.

Duck Egg – The world can be scary sometimes, and though it's easier to stay where it's safe and warm, you struggle to try and break out of your shell.

"Just Ducky" – Everything is going well, and you're a happy go lucky person who doesn't say no to anything, even if you want to.

Wounded Duck – You're not sure what to do with yourself and feel like you have been hurt by so many people in the past.

Donald Duck – You are hot-tempered and can really lose it when things don't go your way.

Daisy Duck – You are devoted to your boyfriend or girlfriend no matter what. Sometimes people have a hard time understanding why you are so attached to your significant other.

Darkwing Duck – You feel the inner struggle between seeking fame and fortune versus putting others before yourself.

More than likely you are a combo of these different types of "ducks." This was a simple warm-up to help you to start thinking about what makes you tick and how you currently view yourself. Our goal in the next chapter will be to take hold of this underwater churning, so we can start to control it. So let's hit the open waters so we can start learning how to navigate those difficult conversations you've constantly been "ducking."

CHAPTER 2

THE TRIPLE BYPASS

Have you ever ridden on an old, rickety wooden roller coaster? You know, the kind with the chipped, white paint, rusty tracks and wheels, and danger signs posted everywhere? Concentrate on those ten seconds—the ones that seem like they'll last for all of eternity—when you are being pulled up to the highest peak of the coaster. Your fingers grip tighter on the bar, perspiration is leaping from your pores, and your heart feels like it's going to beat right out of your chest. At the same time the conversation you are having with yourself is going completely off the rails. *How old is this thing? What was that sound? Oh man, why the heck did I agree to this? I want to get off! Oh crap, I can't get off.* You start imagining how many people will show up to your funeral. (You'd like to think at least a couple hundred or so.) Then all of a sudden the coaster stops! *Wow that's a pretty view,* you think, looking out over the rest of the theme park and the surrounding area for a moment before you remember just how high up you are. Maybe your fear returns, and you just *know* that you're a goner. Then you summit the peak, and as the coaster car drops and that weightless feeling takes over, you feel your heart jump up into your throat.

This roller coaster of emotions is exactly what we go through when we're about to have a difficult conversation. Don't worry, it's not just you. Difficult conversations are flat out deadly, and the fear leading up to and during them is paralyzing to a majority of people. But why are these scenarios so much more complicated than the millions of other conversations we've had throughout our lives? Why do we freeze up or get defensive when it comes to tackling tough topics? Well, difficult conversations have a tendency to attack us at the very heart of who we are. This allows fear to seep in through our valves and then circulate throughout our entire system. But if we could just take a step back and approach these conversations from a clinical, almost surgical standpoint, we could rock these tough talks like they're nothing more than a casual chat with a friend. Doesn't that sound better than the mental chaos you feel when a parent, teacher, or friend says those dreaded words: "We need to talk"?

The Triggers of Our Own Personal Heart Attacks

Before I can teach you to pick up that figurative scalpel, we need to first complete a diagnosis of what triggers you to flip out, shut down, or tear up during a difficult conversation.

Do you lose your mind on your parents when they try to give you advice you don't want or agree with?

Do you hide from or give in to the "popular" kid at school because you are afraid of the backlash if he doesn't agree with you?

Is your best friend spreading nasty rumors all of a sudden that are sending you into a mental and emotional spiral?

Did your teacher give you a lousy grade and you have no idea why?

Are you struggling to find a way to tell your close friend you think their boyfriend is a jerk without destroying your friendship?

Think about what these questions all have in common. They are all an attack on you.

Or are they?

You're a human being, and that means you have emotions and insecurities. Don't say that you don't, because that is just a big fat lie you are telling yourself. You have grown up in a culture where it is not okay to show these insecurities so you do an excellent job of hiding them. Remember that duck who looks to be gliding on top of the surface but is actually churning up the water like crazy underneath? Here's the truth: The most successful people—whether it comes to relationships, business, sports, or life in general—are aware of and can name their insecurities and weaknesses. Believe it or not, this awareness is actually super empowering when it comes to having difficult conversations.

Think back to the example of your parents giving you advice you don't want or need. What is it, really, that makes you shut down while they talk to you? Is it that they don't understand your life and where you're coming from, or that you feel like they don't believe you can handle this situation on your own? If you don't stop to think about what it is that's upsetting you, the conversation can quickly go off the rails, like a locomotive that crashes and burns in a fiery explosion the second it leaves the tracks. But if you can train yourself to keep a keen eye out for when and how these insecurities are being triggered, you'll find that eventually you can keep the locomotive on the tracks and heading in the right direction. You might even find that, with a little bit of practice, that train will reach its destination every time, without any trouble.

My Big Fat Lie

Let me tell you a story, but first I need to give you a little background. The conversation I am about to share with you took place between my dad and me when I was sixteen years old. I had just gotten my license a few weeks before, and I borrowed my dad's car to go play soccer with a friend. Or so he thought. What actually happened is that I lied and went to visit my girlfriend, Mandy, at her friend's house instead. It was foolproof, I thought, but that was before I got caught. Like an idiot, I locked the keys in the car, and I was forced to fess up and tell my dad where I really was so he could bring me the spare set.

My dad was furious when I called him. He is not someone you want to piss off and definitely not someone you want to lie to. Growing up, my friends referred to him as the "silent assassin." He may be a man of small stature and few words, but his glare can absolutely kill you. I could just picture him on the other end of the line, his face beet red, steam coming out of his ears, and that ice cold stare in full effect.

My dad sent my older sister Erin to drop off the spare set of keys, and she reamed me a new one when she arrived. I drove home with a thick knot of dread in my throat. I knew I was in for it. Sure enough, when I pulled into the driveway and walked up to the front door of my parents' house, my dad was waiting for me.

"I can't believe you lied to me," my dad yelled, fuming. "We are so disappointed in you. You're grounded."

"Grounded?" I asked in disbelief. "For what? I told you I was going to play soccer with a friend—I never said where. I played soccer."

"With who? Mandy?"

"No," I said forcefully. "With her friend, who is going D-1 to play soccer next year." I thought the detail would help me in my defense. Spoiler alert: it didn't.

"We trusted you." My dad shook his head in disappointment, and I felt the knot in my throat sink to my stomach, where it sat like a heavy weight holding me to the floor. "You're grounded for two weeks."

I rolled my eyes. There was nothing I could say that would change his mind, and I could feel the heat of my shame turn to anger. "Fine," I said angrily. "I don't care. I know you hate Mandy anyway!" I pushed past my dad into the house and stomped upstairs to my room, slamming the door behind me.

I want to dissect this difficult conversation with you because the truth is, if I had the skills that I am about to teach you it could have gone very differently. This whole conversation—and my lie—could have been completely avoided. Let's take a look at what triggered me to react the way I did.

Look at the first sentence. What word do you see my dad using multiple times? That's correct. The word "you." When my dad used this word it immediately triggered my fight-or-flight instinct and at your age, I always chose fight. I felt attacked. He went right after my character, which I had been diligently building for sixteen years. I had never lied to them before. Maybe a few fibs and stretches of the truth, but never a flat out lie like I did that day. It hurt me to feel that a single transgression on my part had made him so angry and wiped out all the hard work I had done over the years to be a good son. That leads us to the next trigger? Why did I feel the need to lie?

Read the conversation through again and see if you can figure out what the underlying trigger is. Think you have it? Here's a hint: it's in the last line. I thought my parents hated my girlfriend Mandy, a person I cared a lot about. I'm sure some of you reading this book can relate to this. Let me give you a little more background.

During my sophomore year, I started for my high school's varsity soccer team after playing JV the previous year. I literally practiced every single day to make the varsity team; in the winter, I even shoveled my backyard after snowstorms so I'd have space to practice. My dad was so proud of me for my hard work and perseverance. By my third game in, I had already racked up multiple points. I was on top of the world, and the team loved me. Then I broke my collarbone during the fourth game and everything I worked for was ripped away.

I was super quiet in school and not much of a risk-taker. I would talk to girls if they talked to me first but never even entertained the idea of asking one out. I was stressed out from school and life in general, and my one outlet—soccer—was gone. Then Mandy popped into my life. For the first time since my injury I felt happy, and it was finally something other than soccer causing it.

When Mandy and I started dating, we spent all of our free time together. We'd go out on weekends and after school, and soon, the pain and frustration of no longer being able to play soccer was a distant memory. I stopped training to come back from my broken collarbone, and my dad began to notice my focus, once so disciplined and single minded in my soccer aspirations, turn instead to dating a girl who dropped a four letter word in front of my parents on her first visit to my house. I know, I can't say it was the best first impression.

I'm about to get deep on you for a second. We all have a desire to be needed, accepted, and loved. I stopped feeling that from soccer after my injury, and Mandy began to fill that void. My dad, on the other hand, saw her as a negative distraction and as a bad influence on my life. Do you always see eye to eye with your parents? Nope, me neither.

But let's get back to my triggers. To recap: the first trigger was feeling as though my dad was attacking the integrity of my character. The second trigger was believing my dad hated Mandy, the person who was fulfilling my need for acceptance and love. So what both these triggers boiled down to was me protecting my identity, my ego, and who I believed I was.

Your Identity

Remember that little warm-up about deciding what type of duck you were? Now it's time to dig a little deeper. If you want your next difficult conversation to go well, this is where you need to buckle down and put in some effort. Grab the crinkled piece of paper you just threw out and the pencil you snapped in half while doing your math homework. I want you to write down each header below and write down what it is asking for. Yeah, yeah, I know, you have enough homework already, but bear with me. This little activity could end up making your life easier (not easy but easier). Honestly, it's gonna blow your mind. It'll take you five minutes and could save you from hours and hours of future headaches.

Three Positive Words You Know That Describe You. (Be honest.)

Three Negative Words You Feel Describe You. (Remember, you're the only one seeing this.)

Three Words Your Best Friend Would Use to Describe You.

Three Words Your Worst Enemy Would Use to Describe You. (This may hurt a little bit, but if you apply the strategies in this book they may end up being someone you get along with.)

Three Words Your Family Members Would Use to Describe You.

Three Words Your Teachers Would Use to Describe You.

You just skipped this part, didn't you?!

For your own sake, go back and do it. I'm trying to help you out here!

Why did I ask you to do this little exercise? To find what we are looking for—YOUR IDENTITY. The way you view yourself is splattered across your page now. We all have a certain idea of who we are and how the world sees us, and this forms our identity. We, as human beings, often want to be seen as flawless. We have an idea of who we are and we don't want anyone to take that away from us. So what do we do? We hide our flaws from the outside world and do our best to project only those things we think will be seen as admirable. But sometimes outsiders find a way into the deepest, most-treasured parts of our hearts and souls. And when they do, it can be all too easy to worry that they might find a flaw in that most precious part of our being that no one is supposed to touch: our identity.

I want you to specifically search for the words on your paper that trigger your sense of identity. Make note of the words that make you angry, make you feel like crap, make you defensive, or make you want to hurt the person saying them. Let me tell you something. These triggers hurt and there's a reason they set off fireworks.

Maybe the 'mean girls' at school are spreading rumors about you that aren't true (attack on identity). Maybe your teacher embarrassed you in front of the class and basically called you stupid (attack on identity). Maybe your parents are continually calling you lazy and a waste of space (attack on identity).

If you're still having trouble figuring out what your triggers are, answer these next two questions:

In your last difficult conversation, what made you enraged or hurt?

What are the two things you are most insecure about?

Answer these questions and you should have a pretty good idea of what is going to set you off in a conversation. Once you have these triggers in mind, you can start to work on controlling them so they don't affect you so much.

Let me show you the power of knowing your triggers. I am going to rewind to the same conversation with my dad, except this time I know my triggers going in. If my dad hits one of my triggers, I am not going to allow myself to become defensive or enraged. I am going to navigate through it.

"I can't believe you lied to me," my dad yells, fuming. "We are so disappointed in you! You're grounded!"

I take a deep breath and remind myself that my dad doesn't know the whole story. "You're right," I say calmly. "I did lie to you, and you have every right to be disappointed in me. I'm curious if you know why I felt I had to lie to you instead of telling you the truth?"

My dad said the same exact line to me, only this time I didn't let his full-frontal attack trigger my insecurities about my character. How do you think my new line would have changed this conversation? If I had responded this way instead of getting defensive, I might have moved the conversation in a drastically different direction, one that would have been much more productive and resulted in what both my dad and I wanted: mutual understanding.

Understanding how I could have changed my response to my dad unlocked something in me; it's something that has since become the first step to my CPR Method. Through CPR, I've learned to confront and control my emotions and insecurities during difficult conversations, and believe it or not, it's easier than you think.

CHAPTER 3

CURIOSITY

Curiosity

P

R

"Curiosity will conquer fear even more than bravery will."

—James Stephens

I t may have killed the cat but sure as heck, curiosity is going to be a lifesaver for you. The first key to unlocking any difficult conversation is to take a standpoint of curiosity. Most of us get so revved up about how we feel and our thoughts about the situation that we completely forget about the other person. Well, I've got news for you. It takes at least two people to have a difficult conversation, and the majority of the time we think we know what the other person is thinking or feeling. We usually end up being a little bit further off the mark than we thought, and sometimes we even miss the mark entirely. It's completely natural to think about yourself in a conversation, but if you can learn to take a standpoint of curiosity about the other person, it's going to be a game-changer for you.

Step 1: Listen, Listen, and Oh Yeah... Listen Some More

A lot of people believe they are really good listeners. The truth is, a few of us are, but most of us are mediocre listeners at best. Why, you ask? Often because the other person is talking about themselves. Like I stated before, we naturally focus on ourselves. It's not uncommon to zone out during a conversation, waiting for the other person to say something you can relate to so you can turn the conversation to yourself. The other person might even be doing the same thing. This is totally normal, but it's not usually the most productive way to speak with someone.

But when you actually *listen* to the other person's viewpoint or story, you'll find they are providing you with information you can use as an entry point to help you turn that difficult conversation in a direction that makes both people happier. Why should you want to make the other party happy? Well, because then that conversation will become a lot less difficult for *you*. Think back on the list you wrote about your identity. When your parent or teacher is upset with you, or you're having a difficult conversation with a friend, you should listen to what they're saying to try and discern the triggers on *their* list: their underlying fears, concerns, ways in which they felt hurt, the things you did right, and their identity triggers. If you can master the skill of listening you are well on your way to dominating a difficult conversation.

Think about this: we were given two ears and one mouth. This is in proportion to exactly what we should be doing in a tough conversation: twice as much listening as compared to talking. This is going to take some work but it will no doubt pay dividends later.

Step 2: Take the Feedback

Another reason we struggle with listening to others is because we flat out don't like what they are saying. Maybe they are spewing out verbal diarrhea that you just want to deflect, or maybe what they have to say goes against what you want to do or how you view yourself. This turns us off and we struggle to stay tuned in. Often while we are in the process of listening, the other person may be making a bunch of "you" statements, just like my dad did in my example. No one wants to be told how YOU feel, YOUR intent, YOUR actions, and what YOU should do to fix it, so it can be pretty darn hard not to defend yourself. But I'm telling you right now, keep listening and absorb the feedback. This often means biting your tongue, shutting your yapper, and just flat out taking it all in. I never said it was easy.

Let me tell you what I have always noticed during or after every difficult conversation I have ever been a part of. I have always discovered at least one nugget of truth from that person's mouth that I can walk away with, and which helps refine who I am. It might be that I contributed to a problem in a way I had no clue about. It might be that I thought I was listening when actually this person was hurt because they could easily tell I had no interest at all. Or maybe a person I'm close to tells me a trigger they have that I had no idea existed. Being able to take feedback is another skill and you need to be able to accept it whether it's good, bad, or flat out ugly. You need to be curious about that feedback and dissect the information that is useful and helpful to you. Trust me, you'll be able to get your thoughts and feelings in later but do it in a more purposeful and tactful way because of the feedback you were able to absorb.

Step 3: Acknowledge and Make It Safe

Remember we have taken a standpoint of curiosity. In Step 1, I asked you to listen for the other person's fears, concerns, identity triggers, underlying feelings and thoughts. In Step 2, you gathered the feedback. Here's where you need to use the new information. You now need to acknowledge these fears, concerns, and triggers you discovered from your counterpart.

The reason is threefold:

a) **You demonstrate to the person you were listening and genuinely taking interest in what they had to say.**

Example: "What I hear you saying is that you really want to play on the baseball team, but my friends and I have been riding you pretty hard lately and ruining the game you love to play."

What most people really want is to be heard. Sometimes this alone can solve the entire problem. Often, you just need to show them you care about what they have to say.

b) **You make the conversation safe to continue.**

Example: "It sounds like you were the target of a lot of short jokes during elementary school. I can see how that would upset you now when I call you 'shorty.'" (I can relate to this one. When I was a freshman in high school I was a massive five foot one!)

My senior year in high school I took AP Psychology and I only remember two things: Pavlov's dogs and Maslow's hierarchy of needs. Maslow made it clear that people absolutely need safety before they are ready to process feelings. While you were listening in steps 1 and 2, this person most likely put themselves out there and risked parts of their identity. You need to reward them with safety if you want them to proceed and work toward an agreement or resolution.

c) **You give the other person a reason to retract their claws.**

Example: "If I hear you correctly, you worked really hard on getting a solid A on this project and as your partner I really didn't hold my weight. I totally agree with you and want to make right by it."

In a heated conversation, the last thing a person expects you to do is agree with them. This takes them off the attack or defensive and puts them in a place where they will be open to hearing what you say. Don't just agree with anything, but agree on something you feel is true. If you were being a knucklehead, then agree you were being a knucklehead.

Let's go back and take a look at the new conversation I was beginning to have with my dad.

"I can't believe you lied to me," my dad yelled, fuming. "We are so disappointed in you! You're grounded!"

"You're right," I said calmly. "I did lie to you, and you have every right to be disappointed in me. I'm curious if you know why I felt I had to lie to you instead of telling you the truth?"

What did I accomplish with these two lines? Let's look at my first sentence. My dad stated that I lied to him and that he was disappointed in me. During the new conversation, I agreed with him, and then demonstrated I was listening to what my dad was saying by repeating the words he used such as "lie" and "disappointment." (Luckily for me, my dad is a man of few words. Some of you guys probably have parents that will go on forever, and unfortunately for you, you just have to suck it up and listen.) I also took the feedback that was coming my way. Do you think I liked being called a liar? And we all know one of the worst things your parents can say to you is that they're disappointed in you.

When the original conversation took place, I got defensive about this statement and tried to squirm my way out of the lie. In the new conversation I used his feedback to acknowledge that I was listening and to admit I'd messed up. This moved the conversation exactly to where I wanted it. My dad was gearing up for a fight, but I acknowledged that I was wrong for lying and agreed his feeling of disappointment made sense. Don't you think that would make him let down his guard a bit?

Now I want you to turn your attention to my second sentence, because it is just as important as the first. My dad was obviously mad at me but I really wanted him to understand my point of view. In order to do this, I couldn't just tell him why I lied. He would have said, "Well, you could have told me that instead of lying." But then he obviously wouldn't understand how he made me feel I had no choice but to lie. So the best way to my dad's enlightenment was to indeed take a standpoint of curiosity in order to understand his thinking. At the same time, my hope would have been that my curiosity would inspire his own; maybe he could have come to terms with the fact that he was contributing to the problem as well.

And with that, it sounds like we are moving on from the C to the P of the CPR Method.

CHAPTER 4

PURPOSE

Curiosity
Purpose
R

> "When you dance, your purpose is not to
> get to a certain spot on the floor.
> It's to enjoy each step along the way."
>
> —Wayne Dyer

When you enter into a difficult conversation, it's important to have an intention. Do you want to make the other person see your point of view? Are you trying to impart a specific piece of information? Knowing your purpose before engaging in a difficult conversation can make or break its overall success.

Step 4: Turning a Difficult Conversation into a Learning Conversation

When most people are involved in an argument, their objective is to "win" that argument. I sure felt this way for the majority of my life, and while maybe there is a place for this in actual debates, there definitely is not when it comes to life's difficult conversations with family members, friends, teammates, or peers. If you approach a difficult conversation with an end-goal of winning, then you totally just lost. Someone is going to end up with more polarizing feelings, more hurt, more hate, and more of a reason to complicate this difficult conversation even further. Remember I've been a coach, teacher and assistant principal for a decade now, and I've seen time and again the pain and suffering caused by the 'I'm going to win and you're going to lose' approach.

Another attitude people go into a difficult conversation with is that they are going to CHANGE the other person. This is virtually impossible. You cannot change who a person is. Trust me. I've tried to change people to be more like me or more like how I want them to be. It never works. The only way a person can be changed is if they do it themselves. That person can be inspired by you, guided by you, led by you, or criticized by you, but that doesn't necessarily mean that person is going to change. The only way a person can change is on their own, by the choices they decide to make. Don't go into a difficult conversation to change the other person. It will blow up in your face.

Your goal should be to turn the difficult conversation into a LEARNING conversation by focusing on trying to understand the other person's point of view. Clearly if you are in a heated disagreement then you either misunderstood one another, don't see eye-to-eye on something, or somebody's triggers were set off. Doesn't it make sense then to learn about the thinking and perspective of the other person? Doesn't it make sense to learn about what triggered their volcanic eruption? Don't you want them to see from your point of view, and learn about what you were thinking and why you took those actions? This doesn't mean you will both agree on everything but at least it will help you to begin seeing through the lens of the other person instead of just your own. Learning about each other's perspectives is a pivotal mindset to have in order to be successful in any difficult conversation.

Step 5: Express Your Thoughts and Feelings in a Productive Way

The first part of the difficult conversation was taking a standpoint of curiosity by listening, taking the feedback and making acknowledgements so that the other person felt heard. Now that we are in the learning part of the conversation you need to make sure you express your own thoughts and feelings, too. This is important so you feel heard as well and you don't leave the conversation without the other person learning more about you and your perspective.

Here are three tips to use when you are expressing yourself:

Tip #1: Don't tell the other person their intent or what they were thinking.

Think about how you feel when someone tells you what YOU are, or what YOU feel. You hate it. Remember that! The exception to this rule is when the other person has already told you their perspective during your listening session.

Tip #2: Use "I feel…" statements.

Example: "I felt pretty hurt when you called me stupid at the lunch table in front of all of our friends."

Instead of: "You are a jerk for calling me stupid in front of everyone! You are trying to take away all my friends and don't care about anyone but yourself!"

Tip #3: Feelings vs. Facts

I interview students, teachers, and parents all the time in my job and I have noticed one consistency. The real truth usually lies somewhere between both people's point of view. It is my job to really act on the facts so I have become skilled at sorting out feelings and opinions versus what actually happened. This is super important because in a difficult conversation you can always agree upon the truth, not on feelings. Feelings are hard to interpret and when you accuse the other person of trying to hurt yours it's going to get messy and may not be accurate.

Entering into a difficult conversation without purpose doesn't make any sense at all. How can you expect the conversation to go smoothly if you don't even know what direction you want it to go? The purpose is not to 'win the argument' or 'fix the other person.' If you begin an interaction with these mindsets you can be sure whatever is going on is going to get worse, not better. The purpose of a difficult conversation is to *learn*. You need to learn about the other person. What made them say that? What made them do that? What did I ever do to them to deserve this? Come at it with curiosity and know that your purpose is to learn.

Now that you've learned the C and the P, it's time to wrap it up with the R.

CHAPTER 5

REFLECTION

Curiosity
Purpose
Reflection

"Learning without reflection is a waste.
Reflection without learning is dangerous."

—Confucius

E very morning most of you look at your reflection in the mirror in your bedroom or while you're getting ready in the bathroom. You're looking at how you appear on the surface. Is every piece of hair in place? How do I cover up this enormous red zit on my face? Does this shirt look good on me? Are people going to make fun of me? As you do this, you are analyzing how you see yourself and perceive how others will see you. In other words, you are reflecting on your reflection.

Reflecting on difficult conversations is a similar process. On the surface you have some issues you just want to get rid of. Let's compare this to a zit on your face. It's angry, it's red, and it comes across as nasty. What you really want to know is how to get rid of it. To do so, you'll need to address the underlying issue that is causing it. The same thing is true for a difficult conversation. There is an underlying issue (sometimes more than one) that is causing this conversation to be difficult. Companies like Clean & Clear have already figured out how to treat your zit problem, so let's take a look at how reflection will fit into treating and even possibly dissolving the underlying issues at the root of your difficult conversations.

The Two Things You Need to Be Able to Reflect

#1: Time

When I first started as a young math teacher (I was closer in age to you than I was to most of the other teachers in my department), I was observed by my department head, Mrs. Smith. It's obviously nerve-wracking when your boss is looking at your every move, and I felt anxious the entire time, constantly aware that she was sitting in the corner with her clipboard, watching me. The day after my observation I met up with her and she gave me some advice that completely changed my classroom. She hit on everything I was doing well and then gave me one piece of simple advice.

She said to me, "You need to give students more time."

It floored me, but the more I thought about it, the more I realized she was right. In my class, I would ask students questions and rush their thought processes without giving them enough time to process the information. How could they possibly put into practice the methods they had only just learned and formulate a correct answer if they didn't have time to put thought into it? The very next day, I began to experiment, pushing myself to give my students extra time to think, and the results were amazing. I began to notice more students were participating in discussions, and not only that, but the quality of answers increased as well. Once, I waited four, dead-silent minutes for the class to answer a particularly challenging question. Imagine sitting in that class. Once the fourth minute hit, 22 out of 25 hands had gone up. Time, I quickly realized, is a game-changer!

Time is crucial in order for you to unpack the amount of information that comes at you in a difficult conversation. In these types of scenarios, you need time for your brain to process what is happening and allow it time for an appropriate and purposeful response. The next time you see two people in a heated argument, watch them. Time how fast they respond after the other person speaks. My guess would be that each person responds immediately, maybe even interrupting the other person (with probably not so nice words). They're just spewing out whatever information that is currently at the tip of their tongue without listening or reflecting on what the other person is saying, and the other person is probably doing the same. How's that argument going? I'm going to guess it didn't end so well.

When my wife and I get into a difficult conversation, she wants an immediate reaction from me. I will tell you right now that if you get an immediate reaction from me on a tense topic, it's not going to be productive for you at all and may even sting a little. So what do I do? I wait. I don't answer immediately. I take my time, take the information in, allow myself to be curious about that information, and then I reflect on it and formulate my response. Sometimes this takes five seconds, and sometimes it takes almost a minute, and sometimes my wife feels like this silence lasts for all of eternity. It's true that a long pause during an argument can make the other person feel like you're avoiding the conversation, so sometimes it's best to let them know that you're in the process of reflecting. One line you can use if you need some time is "I just need a minute to take that in and think about that." This is tough stuff and you need to be thoughtful during this conversation. It also means that when it comes time for the other person to respond to your words, you need to be able to give *them* time to think and respond as well.

#2: Mindset

You are at an age where a lot of emotionally-charged things are happening to you, not to mention all those hormonal changes. It's super easy to become angry, upset, or defensive. You need to do your best to keep your emotions in check and make sure you are entering into each difficult conversation with a growth mindset.

Carol Dweck, a super well-known Stanford University psychologist, came up with this terminology of a 'Growth Mindset' after studying students like you: She noticed some students didn't believe they were capable of learning difficult material. Other, more confident students *did* believe they could take on the difficult tasks and learn the content. Her studies showed that students who believed they could learn the material were much more likely to grasp the material and "grow their brains" than their counterparts who had a limiting mindset.

You must be in a learning mindset in order to successfully navigate a difficult conversation. If you are not, there will be nothing to gain and reflect upon from having the conversation, and you will probably walk away from it angry. You can use time sometimes to put you back into the right mindset. If someone hits your trigger you may need to ask if you can take a couple minutes to gather your thoughts. There probably will be times in really complex conversations where you'll need to end the interaction and agree to pick it back up at another time. The more difficult conversations you are in, the more control and awareness you will have over your mindset.

What Are You Reflecting On?

Go back to the example of looking at your appearance in the mirror. What are you doing when you are staring at your reflection? Are you asking questions such as, "Is every hair in place?" or "Do I need to change my shirt?" Asking yourself questions like these provide you with an *opportunity* to improve your appearance. The following questions will provide you with opportunities to improve the outcome of your difficult conversation:

1. How are you (Yes, you!) contributing to the issues at hand?
2. What safe questions can you ask the other person to gain more insight? (You need to be curious here!)
3. What misunderstanding is at the root of this conversation?
4. What information do I need to provide to help the other person understand?
5. Are there solutions that would satisfy both our concerns?
6. Do we need to have another conversation?

What Are You <u>NOT</u> Reflecting On?

1. Who is to blame?
2. How do I change the other person?
3. What am I going to do Saturday night?

Reflection is simply giving your brain time to go through a meaningful thought process in order to realize the insights and gains you have made from the information you have taken in. You will be amazed at the ideas, thoughts, and solutions that pop into your head just by taking the time to reflect. If you skip this part of the CPR process then you may have just thrown away the solution to a problem or situation that has been sucking up your time and energy. Take the time now to reflect and save yourself the headache later.

CHAPTER 6

LET IT FLOW

The Four Valves You Can't Forget About

As you may have learned in biology class, the heart is a magnificent organ. You probably remember the four chambers of the heart: the left and right atrium and the left and right ventricle. If it's been a couple years since your last biology class, or if you haven't even taken biology yet, you might not know or remember the four valves in the heart: the tricuspid, mitral, pulmonary, and aortic valves. These valves keep your blood flowing in the right direction. One leaky or broken valve can result in inner turmoil.

The same holds true for the four valves in difficult conversations. You want to keep the conversation flowing in the right direction. If you forget about any of the four valves below, your conversation could end up heading the wrong way, where it could lead to a blockage.

Valve 1: Check Your Blind Spots

After a long day of teaching math I used to pick up some extra cash as a driving instructor. Instead of teaching the wonderful world of calculus, I taught students how to do a three-point turn, parallel park (everyone's nemesis), and back up in a straight line. There were only two points in my driving instructor life where I thought I was going to die: Once when a student ran through a stop sign in a four-way intersection (Thank God I had a brake on my side!) and the second was a memorable incident on the highway.

The day started like any other. I pulled into a student's driveway (let's call him Harry) for his last hour of driving instruction. He came out looking disheveled and pretty pissed off. I asked him if everything was alright and he said, "Yeah, I'm fine. Where are we going?" I asked him if he had driven on the highway yet and he let me know he hadn't. He seemed to perk up a bit.

He did a nice job merging smoothly into highway traffic from the on-ramp. We were cruising at the legal limit, a cool 65 miles per hour. Then, BAM! All of sudden Harry went absolutely rogue. He started speeding up and it seemed like he was taking his anger out on the pedal. I calmly let Harry know we needed to slow down and obey the speed limit, but he was cocky and mad—not a good combination—and he ignored me. I could see him checking his mirrors and knew he wanted to get over to a faster lane. He leaned forward and turned the wheel hard to the left.

But Harry made a crucial life-threatening mistake. Can you guess what it was?

Harry forgot to check his BLIND SPOT!

As he turned the wheel to change lanes, he completely overlooked the white sedan we were about to sideswipe. Luckily, I was there; I instinctively grabbed the wheel and jerked it right pulling us back into the right lane. The other driver laid on their horn and had a few choice words to yell, but luckily everyone was fine.

Just like when you're driving, in a difficult conversation you need to check your blind spots. We each see the world through a different lens, which is pretty crazy when you think about it. The problem is, most of the time we think we see everything the same when in reality everyone has a completely different experience and point of view. You could be working in a group and think the group is dysfunctional when actually *you're* the one causing the problem without even knowing it. You might be acting on what you think are facts without knowing the whole story, just like Harry thought he was safe to pull into another lane without noticing the white sedan. Blind spots are all around us and we need to keep an eye out for them.

Use another person's lens as your mirror. Ask if a comment you made was insensitive to someone who witnessed your conversation. Ask if you overreacted to a classmate just trying to help you out. You want to get better in these types of situations.

You want to try an eye-opening activity to unveil your blind spots? Ask your friends what they think you don't realize about yourself. WARNING: This is not for the faint of heart and you have to be willing to take the feedback they give you without knocking their socks off!

Valve 2: Keep Your Negative Thoughts in Check

You ever get that text at 8 o'clock at night from your best friend, Rachel, that Jen is flipping out because you talked to her boyfriend in the hallway on your way to class? Your heart rate increases, you feel a pit begin to form in your stomach, and your mind starts racing. You think about things you can say to make it better. "He just asked me about our history homework," you could tell her, or "I just wanted to tell him how lucky he is to be with you." (I'm going to guess you probably didn't mean that second one.) Your mind starts pouring out negative thoughts, wondering, *Is Jen going to fight me when I walk into school? Will we end up suspended? Is she going to spread rumors that I was trying to steal her boyfriend? I think I'm coming down with a sore throat. I'm not going to school tomorrow.* In cases like these, it's not Jen who is your enemy; it's your own mind.

When I was in school, I was absolutely notorious for letting my thoughts run wild when I knew there was a difficult conversation ahead of me. My mind jumped to the worst-case scenarios immediately. I didn't sleep the night before and would avoid the conversation the next day at all costs. But once I started using the CPR method, 9 times out of 10 the conversation would go immensely better than I thought it would. I came to the realization that these meandering, negative thoughts were just that: thoughts, nothing more. Most of the time these thoughts are not reality. With a little bit of work, we can begin to acknowledge these thoughts and even learn to let go of them. With the help of your newfound CPR knowledge, your conversation will be easier and go better than expected. You need to stop fixating on the negative and letting it eat you alive. Remember, it's not reality!

Valve 3: The Face Rake

My home region of New England (Massachusetts, specifically) is renowned for its breathtaking fall foliage. People drive across the country to get a glimpse of our sea of vibrantly-colored leaves. Then they drive back to wherever they came from and forget about it. What these people don't realize is that all those pretty little leaves end up on the ground. They make a mess out of the summer lawns people work so hard to keep groomed. By the time the trees are bare and snow begins to fall, there are leaves and twigs everywhere.

I actually don't mind the mess. What I do mind is how it hides another mess. You know, the present that my dog, a rescue pup named Sedona, drops off every morning? Like everything else, it gets covered in leaves, and guess who ends up stepping in it? Me. So what do we New Englanders do? We rake. We remove all the leaves, twigs, and crap (literally) from our lawns, clearing the field again and again for a nice, clean slate.

The same thing applies to difficult conversations. But instead of raking your lawn, you have to learn to rake your face. (Although doing the former as well will definitely earn you some points with the adults in your life.) When you start a difficult conversation most of you have a well-groomed, clean face just like my lawn at the start of autumn, with a neutral expression and emotions in check (notice I said most of you). This is good. Then the other person says something that offends you or you don't agree with. Maybe you don't come right out and ask, "Did you seriously just say that?" out loud, but your face certainly says it for you. Just like when those first leaves start falling like raindrops off the branches onto my lawn, your face is starting to look a little messy. As the conversation continues to get more complex and doesn't quite go your way, your face only becomes more and more like my lawn: covered in debris with Sedona's hot mess resting right underneath the surface.

You aren't sending the right message to your counterpart. Your face is probably saying a thousand words right now that will hinder your ultimate success in this conversation. You need to learn to rake your face of strong emotions. Your face can't be saying, "I hate you," "That's not true," or "I completely disagree with you," or I can guarantee nothing productive will come from your interaction. The problem is, many people have no idea they even do this; it's one of their blind spots.

Next time you're on the phone, move over to a mirror and check your reactions and expressions during the conversation. I bet you'll be surprised how much your face gives away. Ask your parents and friends if you wear your emotions on your face during tough conversations. Most people do. You need to learn to stay curious during the conversation and not see everything the other person is saying as an attack meant to hurt you. Remember the purpose of the conversation is to learn, not to win. Reflect on that for a minute.

Valve 4: Don't Be Afraid to End It

In my high school and college years, there was one thing I was always afraid to do in a relationship and that was to end it. Remember my girlfriend, Mandy? After awhile, I knew deep down that my relationship was no longer working positively for either of us, and yet I always convinced myself that my thinking was wrong. If I just gave it more time, I thought, it would work out and we would be a happy couple again. But hanging on to something you know isn't right never turns out in your favor. This is true for difficult conversations as well.

Difficult conversations are just that—difficult. You need to navigate through it, but there also comes a time when you need to end it. How do you know when you need to end it? When you can tell it's not a learning conversation anymore. Perhaps the other person is being nasty and is no longer open to what's being said. Tempers are at an alarming high and someone's head is going to explode. Maybe a trigger of yours was hit and you're just not ready to continue the conversation. Really difficult conversations usually involve more than one talking session.

Don't be afraid to ask to continue at another time if you realize nothing is getting accomplished. Do this calmly and politely. You may need to agree to disagree on some things. Recap the things you guys agreed upon and learned about each other to end on a positive note.

WARNING: In some cases, the other person may refuse to talk or interact with you again. It may not always be a healthy decision, but it is their right. If it's not imperative, you may need to let this one go and move on despite what you want.

Post-Op

Now you know how to surgically work through any difficult conversation. Throw some courage and experience at the tools I have given you and you will be a master surgeon in no time. These skills will continue to serve you over the long haul called life, and they'll only get easier the more you practice them. As you read on to the next section, we'll discuss some methods and tips for putting a finger on the pulse of our life's purpose.

PART 1 RECAP: THE CPR KEYS TO BEING SUCCESSFUL IN A DIFFICULT CONVERSATION

1. Explore Your Identity and Know Your Triggers

2. Take a Standpoint of **Curiosity**
   - Listen, Listen, Listen
   - Take the Feedback
   - Acknowledge and Make the Conversation Safe

3. The **Purpose** Is to Turn the Difficult Conversation into a *Learning* Conversation

4. Get Your Feelings and Thoughts Out Too!
   - Don't Tell the Other Person Their Intent
   - Use "I feel…" Statements
   - Remember the Difference Between Feelings vs. Facts

5. The Two Things You Need to **Reflect**: Time and Growth Mindset

6. Reflect on:
   - How are you (Yes, you!) contributing to the issues at hand?
   - What safe questions can you ask the other person to gain more insight? (You need to be curious here!)
   - What misunderstanding is at the root of this conversation?
   - What information do I need to provide to help the other person understand?
   - Are there solutions that would satisfy both our concerns?
   - Do we need to have another conversation?

7. The Four Valves You Can't Forget About:
   - #1: Check Your Blindspots
   - #2: Keep Your Negative Thoughts in Check
   - #3: Rake Your Face
   - #4: Don't Be Afraid to End It

PART TWO

GETTING A PULSE ON YOUR PURPOSE

Imagine it is late Friday night, and you just had a stellar night out with your friends. Each of you disperses into your separate cars to head home. You are cruising along on the highway jamming out to your favorite song when you realized you missed your exit. Crap! It seems like it takes all of eternity for the next exit to come up. All of a sudden you hear this titanic "thud." The steering wheel is oscillating back and forth, and your car starts rocking like a rowboat in the middle of the ocean. Your brain is popping off danger signals like fireworks on the Fourth of July. You swerve over to the right lane and veer off the exit right in front of you. A dim street light reveals the entrance to a small side street. You put on your blinker, make the turn, and then slam your car into park.

As you swing your door open, you are hit with a blast of cold winter air. You shuffle around to the front of the car. As you round the hood you lock eyes on the front passenger side tire. You blurt out, "Oh man, I'm screwed. Flat tire." You take a minute to peruse your surroundings. You are enveloped in darkness. Then a "Bang! Bang!" startles you. Your body jolts to attention and you sharply turn around. An old, rusty Jeep just backfired.

Suddenly you realize you have no idea where you are. The eerie neighborhood is giving you the creeps. You pull out your cell phone to call your parents, but you find those two words you never want to see in the upper left-hand corner of your screen: *No Service.* Panic sets in. *What am I going to do?* Desperately, you try to think back to that day in shop class when you learned to change a tire. *Damn, I should have paid attention.* Your best night ever just turned into your worst. You have no idea how you are going to get out of this one.

On the other side of the street you see a guy sauntering down the sidewalk wearing a dark coat and an old, worn-out baseball cap. *Do I ask this guy to help me out? What other options do I have?* You wave him down and ask to borrow his cell phone. He says he doesn't have one. *Who the heck doesn't have a cell phone?*

He sees the spare tire you left leaning against the side of your vehicle. He asks if you need help changing it. "Yes!" you respond emphatically. You know you got lucky.

After the stranger finishes putting on your spare, you shut your trunk with the old, mangled tire inside. You thank the guy a million times as he wanders off. You can't wait to get back home. You put your keys in the ignition and turn the engine over. One more problem. You have no idea how to get back home. You pull out your phone. It's dead. You slam your fist down on the dashboard in frustration.

Finally you decide to drive around until you see the highway. You take a sharp left and then a right at the lights. *I thought the highway was right here...?* You make the decision to pull over into a parking lot. You're hoping your parents left a phone charger in their car you borrowed. No such luck, but when you open the glovebox, out pops the most glorious thing you have ever seen! An old GPS. You plug in the adapter and turn it on. It works! Your home address is the first line under favorites. *Yes!*

This story is a great depiction of how life works. One minute we feel like we are crushing it and then all of a sudden something deflates our tire. We end up in a dark unknown place, unsure how to get back to who we are and who we know we can be. If I were a betting man I would bet each of you is a much better and more productive human when you are happy. When you are not happy (such as when your car breaks down in an unknown location) you start to get angry, and maybe a few of those four-letter words make an appearance. You flip out. Remember those ducks at the beginning of the book? In situations like this, most of us are probably asking, "How the duck did we get here?"

What people are really craving and chasing in this world is happiness and joy. They want a sense of purpose. They want to feel like their heart is on fire. The problem is, only a few of us know how to get there. Luckily, I am one of them.

CHAPTER 7

GPS TO LIFE'S ZEST

"Happiness isn't something you put inside
you. It's already there. Sometimes you just
need someone to help you find it."

—Princess Poppy, *Trolls*

When people are unhappy it typically means that someone or something is blocking their happiness. For whatever reason, that person has lost their way and who they are. As humans we tend to bury our happiness and pile on our negative thoughts, emotions, stress, and sadness until we can't take it anymore. We look outside ourselves to search for happiness. It could be a new car, new boyfriend, new house, new watch, more Instagram followers, or more money. You get the idea. We have all been guilty of seeking things outside of ourselves. In fact, the majority of us continue to do this. How is it working for us?

I would say mediocre at best. Sure, those things we consume, those followers we get, those possessions we obtain feel good...for awhile. But once that feeling wears off, we feel empty again, so we immediately set off to find the next best thing. But it's a vicious cycle; we struggle again and again to feel fulfilled, and when we do, that moment of happiness is fleeting.

What if there was a way to feel positive emotions like joy and happiness every day? I'm not naive to the fact that we will still struggle, and feel sadness and anger. But what if more often than not you could feel happy, alive, inspired, excited? Imagine how your days would change. Imagine the impact you would have on your family, your peers, and your teachers.

The truth is, I've been chasing happiness all my life. There were days, weeks, even years at a time where I thought I found it. I thought I found happiness in a girlfriend, a job, a truck, a house, making six figures, and being named Coach of the Year by a nationally known newspaper...but each time, it was fleeting. Each time, the cycle began again.

That is, until I truly found it.

Michael Singer. That is the name of the man who helped me find that I can turn happiness on just like water with a faucet. I have never met Mr. Singer; I heard him being interviewed on a podcast and was enthralled by his thoughts on living your best life. I went out and bought his book, *The Untethered Soul: The Journey Beyond Yourself.* The book is intense and deeply thought-provoking. Personally, I would never have read it at your age, and I certainly don't expect you to read it now. My point is that I needed someone to help me find what I was looking for.

If you haven't already found it yourself, I am hoping to be that person for you. Let me give you my GPS directions to Life's Zest. Whenever you get lost, or feel turned around, come back to the GPS to Life's Zest. This is my tried and true instrument of happiness. I have kept it simple. If there is nothing else in this book you decide to act on, please act on this.

It will change your life.

Gratitude
P
S

> "You can choose to believe life is happening to you
> or life is happening FOR you."
>
> —Tony Robbins

Life is hard. You get knocked down and you get back up again only to get knocked down again. You start to think, "Why does this always happen to me?" Almost everyone, at some point, ponders that specific thought. Right when you feel you finally have your feet on solid ground someone pulls out the rug from underneath you. What if we are looking at it the wrong way? What if the terrible things happening to us are actually helping us?

My teen years were some of my hardest. When I was twelve, my parents separated, and it rocked my world. I'll never forget the day my mom told me and my sisters. We were shocked, but my emotions quickly grew into a fiery anger. I unleashed my inner demon and said some pretty hurtful things. I felt betrayed. My parents were the rock that I always stood on. How could they do this to us?

When something big happens, it becomes all you can think about. Your life changes in an instant and you have absolutely no control over it. Personally, my shock and anger quickly turned to sadness and sorrow. I was embarrassed to tell any of my friends or their parents.

My parents eventually got back together. Shortly thereafter, I found myself in a room with my mom and a therapist. My mom looked at me and then looked at the therapist. The therapist expressed to me that he and my mom were concerned that I was showing signs of depression. Unable to deal with what they were telling me, I got up and walked out.

Truth is, they were right. I was hurting badly. I was in a bad place in a bad way. I had never had an easy time making close friends, and in middle school, I was an introvert and always nervous about getting picked on, so I didn't rock the boat. I ended up going to a private high school, but it didn't help. I was quiet in classes and in the halls, and I held in so much anger and sadness. I felt like I was invisible.

The only thing I could see going for me was on the soccer field; I made varsity starter my sophomore year. Three games in and I already had a couple points. We were playing our crosstown rivals, and I was dribbling the ball up the right sideline. A defender approached me and gave me exactly what I was looking for, an opening in his five-hole. I slid the ball through his legs and met up with it on the other side. The crowd went ballistic! I should have continued to carry the ball up the sideline but I played to the crowd instead. I let the defender catch up with me. And I did what any cocky fifteen-year-old would do: I megged him again. The crowd roared with laughter. Pleased with myself, I passed the ball up the sideline to my awaiting teammate.

CRACK! Excruciating pain shot up through my body. While the ref wasn't looking, the much larger, stronger opposing defender turned and drove his fist into my shoulder (maybe somewhat deservedly, though it wasn't an excuse for poor sportsmanship). I was carted away by ambulance, and soon learned he had broken my collarbone. My one outlet was stolen from me.

That's right about when I met with my mom and the therapist. They hit a nerve with their concerns, because they were right. There were days when I didn't care what happened to me. I didn't care if I got up or if I came home. It was a very dark time and I didn't see my way out of the cycle.

Luckily I had a few friends that took me under their wing. They got me involved in a couple of clubs that helped focus my energy elsewhere. We spent our time working with disadvantaged students from the nearest public school. A couple nights a month, we volunteered at the local food pantry. Those struggling students and families needed us to bring our A-game because we were the only positive thing they had to look forward to every week. What these people didn't realize is, while I thought I was changing their lives, they were actually changing mine. After a couple months, I found myself climbing out of the dark pit I had fallen into.

Believe it or not, I can honestly say now that I am so grateful to have gone through these experiences. What I couldn't see then was the powerful impact they would have on me and people I would come across in the future. Some of my darkest memories ended up providing me with a deep understanding of what it feels like as a teen to work through things such as parental separation and depression. I can now serve my students so much better and with so much passion, because I get it. I can explain to parents what students are experiencing and what they are feeling because I have been there. I couldn't do any of this as effectively if I hadn't gone through it myself. Let me say that again: I've been there, and I made it through.

Gratitude.

It's real and it's necessary. We need to learn to embrace what we have gone through, where we currently are, and what we have. We are being refined. Almost everyone has heard of the saying, "diamond in the rough." In order for diamonds to become as beautiful and strong as they are, they need to undergo extreme amounts of pressure and heat. Humans are no different. Our experiences turn up the pressure and the heat, and over time, they refine us. Instead of life happening *to* us, it is actually happening *for* us.

Too many people get caught up in the "if only" set of thinking. If only we could afford a vacation home; If only my parents made more money; If only I didn't have to go to school; If only I made the soccer team; If only I had a different teacher; If only I got into that college. If only, if only...

If only people could start finding what they are truly thankful for, then they could start being appreciative and happy with the life they are already living. Your parents, guardians, siblings, and teachers can all tell you until they're blue in the face what you should be thankful for, but talk doesn't typically move people.

Experiences move people (Another one of Mr. Tony Robbins' messages). A couple of days ago, a second grader named Gabriela reached out to me. Gabriela is from another country; I sponsor her so she is taken care of and has the necessities to attend school. In her last letter, she let me know how hard learning is for her, but she's determined to write her own letters. She wants to be a teacher or social worker when she gets older. Gabriela's family couldn't provide for her or her sisters' basic needs or education, so they were forced to give them up. Now, Gabriela lives in an orphanage. She has next to nothing when compared to what most of us have, but every letter she sends me is so filled with gratitude for what she does have. Here is a young girl who is dying to learn and dying to serve. She makes me appreciate each day that I did have parents that could support me. She makes me appreciate the education I did receive and the privilege I have to educate the students around me. She inspires me every morning to look around and appreciate the home where I live and the food I get to eat.

On days where I see through this lens I am always happier. I am always a better person, a better husband, a better son, a better educator, and a better friend. I seek these experiences out because they move me. If you're struggling to find something to be grateful for, go volunteer at a food pantry, nursing home, hospital, or homeless shelter. Connect with the people that work there. Ask them what these people are going through. Give yourself an experience that will move you toward gratitude. I've seen it happen again and again. It works. Experiences move people. Life is truly happening for you, not to you (Thanks, Tony)!

How to Find Your Own Gratitude

1. **Write a letter to someone you have been meaning to thank but never really have**. It could be for something small like holding the door open for you in the hallway, or something as big as forgiving you after you made a mistake. Don't expect anything in return!

Don't have enough time to write a letter? Instead make an effort to say thank you—and mean it—to at least three people per day.

2. **Focus on what you do have, not what you don't have**. If you are having trouble with this, look at those around you that have less. I needed a swift kick in the tuchus on this one, which is why I chose to sponsor Gabriela. It was the best thing I ever did.

3. **Give yourself an experience**. Do something that you are passionate or curious about. It could be volunteering at a soup kitchen, food pantry, or elderly housing. It could be going on a service retreat with your youth group. It could be donating blood at a drive or hospital. It could be going to visit a beautiful place in nature. Opportunities for this are everywhere. You can do this on your own, or with a friend or family member. You need to connect with people or places that are going to impact you. No impact = less gratitude.

Gratitude is a nice, solid foundation to start from, but what happens when the world starts throwing those seismic waves your way? Keep reading if you want to know how to survive and thrive when your life gets shaken up.

CHAPTER 8

THE LAND OF FIRE AND ICE

A year ago I found myself in one of the most magnificent places in the world with our middle school travel club. Iceland was filled with hidden gems we had never seen before. We were driving down a narrow, winding road in our comfy coach bus, as our guide let us know we were in the "Land of Fire and Ice". On our left you could see breathtaking waterfalls pouring over the cliffs, and several miles further down the road we turned our attention to a massive glacier that protruded between the mountains. Our destination brought us past a dormant volcano that had aggressively erupted decades before. We could smell the strong scent of phosphorus as we stepped out of the bus to see the locals bake bread in the ground by a set of hot springs. This was indeed the Land of Fire and Ice.

You could tell our driver, Hans, was a native. He knew every turn and landmark like the back of his hand. He spoke broken English but seemed to be able to sing a couple of well-known American rock band songs. In his past work life he was an esteemed member of Iceland's search and rescue team (fun fact: Iceland doesn't have a standing army). Hans decided to take us to one more famous landmark before we turned in for the day. We pulled into what seemed to be a local convenience mart. I thought, *This is the place we are going after everything we saw today?* Hans smiled and told us to go inside.

After stepping through the doors it appeared to be a small strip mall with shops and a food court. To be honest I was still not impressed. Then in the distance I could hear some of our students laughing and hollering for us to come over. The students had found the earthquake simulator. You put a few coins in the machine, lock the door behind you, and then hold on for dear life. In the same room as the earthquake simulator there was a screen with actual video footage from the convenience store during a real, monstrous earthquake. You could see cans flying off the shelves and people spilling to the ground as the ground shook violently around them.

Turns out the actual fault line between the North American and Eurasian tectonic plates runs right through the store. We shuffled a few steps to the right of the simulator, glanced down at our feet, and spotted a narrow section of plexiglass in the floor. Each of us straddled the fault line (locals call them fissures) with our right foot on one tectonic plate and our left foot on the other. We peered down through the glass to get a glimpse of the actual crevasse between two rigid sheets of earth and rock. Waves of awe and bewilderment splashed across our faces (There are only seven major tectonic plates in the world!).

Gratitude
Present
S

"Do not dwell in the past, do not dream of the future,
concentrate the mind on the present moment."

—Buddha

Have you ever actually tried to do this? Concentrate the mind on the present moment? You can usually do it for all of 10-30 seconds until your thoughts start pushing or pulling you somewhere else. Let's say you're in math class, focused on learning how to derive the quadratic formula. All of a sudden your mind wanders to that argument you had with your best friend during second period. Or maybe your thoughts meander into the future, thinking about the big game you have tonight against your crosstown rivals. Maybe it's because the bell rings or the teacher calls on you, but all of a sudden you snap back to the present. You realize you've been daydreaming for ten minutes and haven't a clue where the quadratic formula comes from. This is exactly how most of our minds work.

Our minds are a lot like the tourists straddling the fissures of Iceland. We have our left foot on one plate (let's call this the past) and our right foot on the other plate (the future). We believe the footing we have is solid and steady. We try to stay balanced between the two plates (our present). But when one of the plates (past or future) start to shake, our attention gets pulled to it. After all, we all want to survive the earthquake we call life. Sometimes a plate gives us a small tug and other times it shakes us violently. Each of these tremblings or tremors shift us right out of our focus on being in the present.

Our lives are made up of all the collective choices we make in the present moment, yet most of the time we aren't even there. I don't know about you, but to me, that is downright scary. It's why many of us have been infiltrated by unhappiness. We never experience living our actual lives in the here and now. Instead, we think about how we will be happy in the future when this or that happens. Or maybe we're contemplating the past and focusing on how everything bad always happens to us. Sometimes our thoughts about the past and future collide so violently there is no room for us to be present. But there's a reason it is called "the present". It is truly a gift that we need to learn to unwrap every day if we want true happiness in our lives.

There is a saying in the business world that time is money. Let's say every single day I gave you $1,440 at the start of the day. You could do whatever you want with it. But at the end of the day your balance would be $0 whether you spent it all or not. Then you get a new $1,440 the next day. I'm curious; how would you spend it?

Why that number? There are precisely 1,440 minutes in each day. How do we use each of those minutes? Do we actually live them or do we throw them away? Do we make a difference with them or take them for granted? Adults in your life want to protect you from this fact I am about to tell you but I think we are doing you a disservice if we don't bring it up. Time is precious and nobody knows how much time we get. We can all get more money if we want it but there is not one person out there that can get more time. Yes, you may be able to extend your time by eating healthy, exercising, and all those good habits. But none of us are guaranteed the ability to extend our time here.

The Short End of the Stick

It's hard to believe, but almost six years ago, I met up with one of my close teammates from college at his apartment. Dressed in dark, somber colors, our reunion was nowhere near as joyful as it should have been as we waited for a friend to meet us. We ducked into our car and headed west on the highway, shaking our heads in disbelief and dreading what we were about to do. After over an hour of driving, we parked our car and met up with the rest of our college teammates waiting on the sidewalk near the funeral home where we had all gathered.

We walked side by side into the funeral home together, all of us in utter shock at the death of our friend, Michael Sprouse, who had passed away in his sleep from a brain complication at twenty-six. His face and photos were all around us, and each picture displayed the ear-to-ear smile that always illuminated every room that he walked into. There were pictures of him in his soccer uniform from when he was a kid. In my eyes he was *still* a kid.

Together, my friends and I reminisced about all the great times we had with Sprouse and how he seemed to touch each one of our hearts in his fun-loving sort of way. He was the little brother I never had, the teammate I always found myself paired up with, and the friend I always gravitated toward. He's one of the only people I know that could touch so many people in such a short amount of time. Michael lived each moment as if it were his last. His approach to life is something I'll never forget.

The Present to Yourself

The world wants you to believe you can't contribute or be happy until you're an "adult," out of college, have a "real" job, are a boss, and the list goes on. It is just a false pretense that many of us believe and don't even challenge. I've seen first-hand that young people such as yourself can challenge and blow up this world view.

Think about a time when you have been truly present in your life. Maybe it was when you first learned to ride your bike without training wheels and you felt like you were flying. Maybe it was on a family vacation. Maybe it was when you absolutely nailed that solo as the guitarist in your band's first concert. That happiness was inside of you. You were in the moment. Nothing was blocking you from feeling that happiness. You weren't in the past. You weren't pondering the future. You were right there in that moment. You felt ALIVE! Close your eyes and go back to that moment for a minute...remember how it felt.

Didn't it feel great? The good news is you can choose (right now) to live more in the present. Take one of my former students, for example. Melissa spent most of her day constrained to a wheelchair, due to a form of muscular dystrophy that causes loss of muscle mass and weakness. If you ever met Melissa though, the last word you would use to describe her is weak. In fact, her strength is incredible. She is a true warrior in every sense of the word. In my time knowing her, Melissa always knew how to dominate her time in the present.

Melissa was a huge fan of a doll company growing up (so were my sisters). She collected a bunch of dolls from the company's line. Over time she realized that there were no dolls with disabilities, particularly one in a wheelchair. She decided to write the company producing the dolls and suggest that one be made. Melissa didn't stop there though. She secured a petition that ended up with over 150,000 signatures. Her petition was featured in major news outlets such as Buzzfeed, CBS, and Oprah Magazine. Melissa has since gone on to speak on the topic of disability awareness alongside a Nobel Peace Prize winner, at the United Nations and at TEDex events. She has even written her own book titled, "Mia Lee Wheeling through Middle School."

And the craziest part is that Melissa did all of this at thirteen years old! T-h-i-r-t-e-e-n!

You can choose to be present. It's hard but I challenge you to take a small part of your day and really commit to it. Be in THAT moment! Let go of your worries and stop thinking about what is going to happen next. Live in the moment right in front of you.

How to be present:

1. **Set intention at the beginning of the day**. When you wake up in the morning (you can also do this the night before) pick two moments in which you are going to intentionally be present during your day.

   Example 1: Your dad has had a really stressful week. When you get home from practice, you are setting an intention to cook supper for him. You are going to sit down with him without your phone to be completely engaged in conversation with him.

   Example 2: You are going to ask Haley to sit with you at lunch today. You guys are friends but you haven't really given her the time of day lately.

2. **Turn down the noise.** This is a challenge. Start with five minutes a day where you can just sit in silence with yourself. It could be in your room, in your car, or in your backyard. Try to focus on something constant like your breathing or heartbeat. When your mind starts to wander come back to it. Turn off all your devices so you aren't distracted. We are just hitting our own "Power Off" button to reset our day. Take notice of how good you feel after. As you practice this more and more, build this time up to ten minutes a day, or fifteen, or a half hour.

3. **Enjoy your burger**. Enjoy the savory taste of the meat (or vegetarian patty). Taste each part. The cheese. The mustard. The ketchup. The pickle. The crunch of the lettuce. Feel the softness of the bun on your tongue (You can do the same with a salad or piece of cake). The point is to slow down and use your senses to be in the moment.

4. **Find your own clouds.** We were meant to exist in nature. Get outside any time you are feeling down or gloomy. Look up at the clouds (or stars at night). Watch them drift by in all different shapes and sizes. Realize you are a small part of such an intricate universe. Breathe in the fresh air. Understand the Earth is rotating and orbiting. Take in the sun or feel the rain. Be in the moment. Be present!

Now that we are committed to being present let's join the C.I.A. in the next chapter to complete our quest in finding life's zest!

CHAPTER 9

WORKING WITH THE C.I.A.

Gratitude
Present
Service

"The best way to find yourself is to lose yourself in the service to others."

—Mahatma Gandhi

When I find myself in a period of unhappiness I often
ask myself this question: "Who am I serving?" If the
answer to this question is the person staring back at
me in the mirror I know I am in trouble. Humans have an urge
and desire to serve. For thousands of years, humans have been
at each other's sides to serve and support one another. It could
be going on a group hunt to secure the village some meat, helping a farmer on a cattle drive, sewing clothing for a neighboring
newborn, or taking care of a widow who lost her husband. We
have continued to evolve and become a more advanced society,

but I think our focus should be on becoming a happier, more connected society. Everyone seems to be chasing the six figure job, five bedroom home, and new car, which are all respectable goals if that is what you want or need. I think the mistake we are making is that we genuinely believe those "things" are going to make us happy. We take it a step further and believe we actually have to work ourselves to death to get there. It's a vicious cycle, one that I'm looking to end.

Instead, let's look at service as the vehicle to get there. Think about the last time you truly served someone. Maybe it was your parents when you picked up your little brother from soccer practice. Maybe it was mowing the lawn for your elderly neighbor. Maybe it was helping out at a local blood drive. Think about how you felt after this. You were upbeat and had more energy than before. You felt accomplished and as though you got some important work done. You felt this positive, gratifying feeling from within. You could feel happiness.

Last summer I had one of the most incredible experiences of my life. I got to work with the C.I.A. We were commissioned to a poorer, mountaintop town in Vermont. There were about thirty of us in total that were a part of the mission. Upon our arrival at homebase we were given a reconnaissance of the area by a local. We were broken down into smaller units and given our assignments.

A little disclaimer for fear of the United States Central Intelligence Agency coming after me: The C.I.A. (Catholics In Action) was the name chosen by our local youth group in one of our local churches. The C.I.A. is made up of teens your age who were ready to take action and make a difference in the lives of others. The energy of this group was electrifying.

We were sent out to serve, and serve we did. We stacked loads of firewood for the elderly and disabled to ensure they would be warm and ready when the snowy winter came (Vermont wood spiders are gargantuan in case you were wondering). We picked hundreds of blueberries to help support a local farm that was struggling to keep up. We emptied a local church attic on a sweltering, sunny day. We weeded the gardens where food was grown and given to the needy. We met some incredible individuals who spoke of turmoil and triumph. We cooked a delicious meatloaf for the hungry at the local food pantry. We were greeted with smiles of joy and appreciation by each person or group we served. No matter how hard the assignment, we were always willing to give 100 percent for the person on the other end.

The mission was transformational. We went in to change these people's lives and we were the ones that came out changed. Our gratitude for what we had in our lives increased dramatically. When we were on our job sites, we were so in the moment and present for that person in front of us that nothing could distract us. We served those people, but we ended up getting so much more in return, because the GPS model is cyclical. One part leads to another, which leads to the other. It goes round and round.

What the Happiest People in the World Do

When I was in my early 20's, I chased money HARD. I started out in a finance job instead of teaching, because the pay was so much better. I became a part of the rat race. Everyone seemed to believe the more money you attained, the happier you would be. Why wouldn't I believe that? The top executives were taking lavish vacations and spending their weekends on yachts. Six months into my job, I realized something. Those top execs were freakin' miserable. Angry. Cold. Pissed off. I couldn't figure out why, but I was miserable, too. I lined up a teaching job for myself (Once you're out of school, you need to pay your bills, after all!) and promptly quit.

Instead of just researching how to make money, I started studying people that were both successful and truly happy. I'm not going to lie. It was hard to find a combination of both. But once I did…JACKPOT! I started poring over all their biographies, books they wrote, interviews they did, and actions they took. And then it finally hit me…

Every single one of them SERVED! Not themselves—others (unlike those miserable top execs). They recognized their purpose was to serve. The funny thing is, the more they served, the more their businesses grew, and the more success they had. They identified where their own personal skills and uncontrollable passion intersected. That intersection is right where they decided to start serving. But they didn't stop there.

People like this have bigger aspirations. They want to set the world on fire. They set bigger and more meaningful goals. Once their goals are established, they identify what skills they need to get there. Then they go get those skills or find someone who has them. No excuses.

How to find your passion and purpose:

1. **What cause, person, group of people, or problem tugs at your heartstrings?**

There's something inside of you that fires you up. Some person or group that you want to help. You may have no idea why. Or maybe you have perfect clarity on this. Personally, I am passionate about orphans. I can't really tell you why it is this group over another. I feel like this passion was planted inside me and there's no way I can ignore it. I want them fed, housed, and given the best life possible!

List your individual, group, problem (environmental, societal, etc.), animal, or cause below:

2. **What skills do you have?**

Are you an incredible artist? Do you know how to write computer code? Can you organize a group event? Are you a skilled listener?

Write down three skills that you currently have:

1.

2.

3.

4. Bonus Skill:

5. Bonus Skill:

3. **What do you want to accomplish in the next 1–3 years?**

Do you want to complete a passion project? Do you want to learn more about a certain population or issue? Do you want to start with a couple small acts before doing something big? Do you want to join a group that is as passionate as you are?

-
-
-

4. **What skills do you need to obtain to make that vision happen?**

Maybe you want to learn how to use a circular saw, so you can build houses with Habitat for Humanity, or learn how to build a website, so you can run a small business. Or maybe you'd like to learn how to use a professional camera, so you can become a skilled photographer.

List three skills you need to obtain:

1.

2.

3.

Now that you have zeroed in on your vision it's important to gain positive momentum. I encourage you to start small. Find your first step toward gaining that new skill or knowledge. Pay close attention to how you feel when you find yourself serving the person or group you listed above. Watch how positively impacting someone else's life will have a profound effect on your own.

CHAPTER 10

POURING GASOLINE ON THE FIRE

I am a massive fan of bonfires, especially on cool autumn nights. There's nothing quite like them—the warmth, the smoky scent, the dancing flames, glowing embers, and the starry sky above. It's beautiful. I have to admit though, sometimes I'm not the best at starting them. There is nothing that frustrates me more, and my wife and family will attest to my breakdowns—and my behavior more suited to a three-year-old than a grown man—when I can't get the fire to ignite.

I have a buddy who is a fireman in his hometown. I've known him since college. He can always ignite a rip-roaring bonfire in a matter of seconds. His key ingredient: accelerant. The fire consumes the reactants more quickly, letting off more heat and light. He always had a knack for getting everyone fired up!

Disclaimer: do not use an accelerant with fire. My buddy is a professional, but messing with fire is extremely dangerous and can lead to extreme harm or even death!

How to Fire Up Your Own Personal Growth

It was the end of a three day conference, and only about fifteen of us were standing in a room of over three hundred people. The presenter had just asked anyone to stand up who made over six figures in the last year. She shot off another prompt. "Remain standing if you are readers." None of us budged. "How many of you read mostly nonfiction?" We all remained firmly standing. Having made her point, she turned her attention to the crowd. The people standing understood how valuable their time was, and had spent that time increasing their skills in order to get where they wanted.

Accelerant #1: Find a Mentor

A mentor is someone who can advise you on your own personal goals. Find someone who is successful at what you want to be doing. They have the knowledge and skills that you need. They can help guide you and save you from an immense amount of frustration and headache. If you want to run a successful plumbing business, find a master plumber with a proven business model and pick his brain. Volunteer to go out on jobs with him or even help him do some paperwork pro bono. Soak up all the knowledge you can. Become the big kahuna of asking the right questions.

Accelerant #2: Read Nonfiction

Congratulations! You are doing this one right now. Reading nonfiction is like having a mentor at your fingertips. You can get extremely valuable information for free at your local library, or for 5-10 bucks online or at your local bookstore. Tap into the knowledge and know-how of an expert. Who knows? Maybe I'll be reading your book one day for some expert advice!

Not a reader? Listen to a podcast. There are thousands of different experts out there across hundreds of genres.

Accelerant #3: The Story You Tell Yourself

Henry Ford's famous quote, "Whether you think you can, or think you can't, you're right," has proven to be pretty darn accurate in my life as well as throughout history. Olympic athletes, top executives, rappers, entrepreneurs, and people from all walks of life have riveting stories to tell you about their heroic journeys from point A to point B. Practically every successful person alive has dealt with epic struggles, and they have managed to come out on top.

If you don't write your own story, the world will write you one. I don't know about you, but I want to be in charge of my own story. Visualize yourself living your best life, your biggest dream. Tell yourself you are going to get there. See each day as a small step closer to something you want to achieve. Know people will try to drag you down and there are a million people that will tell you what you can't do or that you aren't good enough. That's their story, not yours.

The Massive Opportunity for You

I was recently talking to the CEO of a medical tech start-up company. He found out I was a school administrator working with teens. He asked me the million dollar question I always get, "How do you deal with this generation of teens?" I smiled, waiting for him to go off on a tangent. *I'm going through them like water. They want more vacation time before they have even added any value. They go home before project deadlines are completed. It's insane...* I hear it all the time. But this time it was different.

He changed the direction of the conversation. The next words he uttered were for *you*, not me. "There is a massive opportunity for people of this generation. We want to mentor them and train them to be successful. There is so much opportunity for them." Young, intelligent, hard-working people. Massive demand. Massive opportunity. FOR YOU. I told him there are plenty of you out there. If you have read this far into the book you are one of them. Continue to ask yourself, "Who do I want to serve?" and "What skills do I need?" Do this, and you'll go far, both in your career and your personal goals. It's a mutual relationship. It should be give and take.

The Ultimate Inhibitor of Happiness

I'm currently in the camp that there are really only two drivers of human decision-making. The first one is FEAR. (We'll discuss the second one in the next section of the book.) Fear can actually be a good thing. It's what saves you from being mauled by a mountain lion you just spotted on the ridge or the bear banging around in the woods. But how often are we really in life-threatening situations? For most of us, it's actually very rare, yet fear always seems to be seeping into our minds.

More often than not, fear is the ultimate blocker of happiness. Fear entangles itself in your thoughts and emotions. The more energy you give fear, the more it will take over your life. Give it enough and it will paralyze you. Fear of what others will think, say, or do. Fear of failure. Fear of what is going to happen next. Fear of losing control. Fear of the unknown, the misunderstood, or the stereotypes. Fear will swallow you up and spit you out if you let it. (It is also an excellent opponent at freeze tag. Just sayin'!)

Substitution

As a former math teacher I have to go here: systems of equations. Many of you just cringed, but hang on for a second. As you know from your algebra class, there are multiple ways to solve a system of equations including by graphing, elimination, or substitution.

When you were first learning to solve systems of equations and had the opportunity to use any of the methods mentioned above, you typically chose substitution. Why? It made sense to you. You would isolate the variable and 'substitute' the newfound value or expression for that isolated variable into the other equation.

Overcoming fear works in the same way. You need to isolate your negative or fearful thoughts and substitute them with more positive ones. Just like solving a system, this takes practice. Some of you will be able to do this on your own and some of you may need to ask a teacher, parent, or counselor for help.

Let me give you an example:

Negative Thought (backed by fear): I'm not going to ask my question in physics because everyone is going to think I am dumb.

Positive Substitution: I am going to ask my question in physics. I am here in school to learn and if I have this question I bet other people do, too. I'm going to ask it and if someone makes a negative comment, I'm going to ignore them.

1. **What are two people, ideas, things, or thoughts you are fearful of?**
2. **How do those fears hold you back?**
3. **Pick one fear holding you back. What do you need to overcome it?**

Examples could be:

I need to read a book on how to build my confidence.

I need to learn how to let go of what others think of me.

I need to work with a counselor on how to stop thinking so negatively all the time.

I need to have a difficult conversation with my parents about...

I need to learn more about this culture so I understand...

4. **What is one fearful thought you would like to replace? What can you replace it with?**

Now that we know what can speed up or slow down our success and happiness, we need to visit what happens when we get a little too big for our britches. I can't think of a better way than to share with you my own disasters in home renovation.

CHAPTER 11

THE RIGHT TOOLS FOR THE JOB

Smash! Shower tiles came crashing down into the bathroom tub. My attempt to balance myself ended with my hand piercing through the soggy, dilapidated, purple-tiled bathroom wall. Staring at the gaping hole in disbelief, I quickly turned off the water and hopped out of the shower. What was I going to do? I had recently bought an older home and was strapped for money.

I called my buddy Toph. He had plenty of experience as a handyman doing all different types of construction projects. He freed himself up to come over and assess the damage. He took one look at it and said, "You have to gut it. The wall is disintegrating." At this point in my life I had no money and certainly no skills in the construction arena. He reaffirmed that he would help get me started and that I could do the majority of the work.

Let's just say there was a steep learning curve for me. I grew to appreciate the hands-on learning experience I was getting and have to say I thoroughly enjoyed smashing those tiles and tearing down the walls. Toph got me started with putting up a cement backer board to replace the torn-down walls. He gave me a quick demo on how to tile and I was off to the races! I'm not sure if my pace was that of a tortoise, snail, or sloth, but you get the idea. Despite the time suck, I stuck with it and wouldn't let anything stop me.

I actually learned a ton and my skills got sharper and sharper. I gutted the three remaining walls and decided to apply my new skill sets to the rest of the upstairs bathroom. Not to toot my own horn but I was getting pretty good at this construction stuff. My confidence grew and I felt like I was unstoppable!

Swiss Cheese

I was wrapping up the area around my shower and needed to nail up some trim next to the tiled shower and tub. I picked up some trim at the local hardware store, measured the length of the needed area, and then the length of the trim piece I had bought. The trim piece was too long. Darn it! I had a couple of special cuts I needed to make but I didn't have the proper tools to make it.

Cocky me decided I didn't need those tools. I'd get the job done just fine without them—there was no stopping me. I whipped out my trusty utility knife and started carving away right there in the bathroom. The top came out picture perfect. I could feel the blade was becoming a bit dull so I decided to change it before my next cut.

With a fresh new blade attached I was ready to make a more challenging cut in the trim that would hug the curve of the tub. Thinking it was going to be a tough cut I held the base of the knife tightly, touched the tip of the blade to the trim and cut into the piece with an immense amount of pressure.

I completely miscalculated! The new blade sliced through the medium density fiber like swiss cheese. I was thrown off balance and my hand slipped. Completely startled, I looked at both hands and made sure I could count five fingers on each. All good.

I went to grab the piece of trim again with my left hand, and saw something red begin to pour all over the trim. I flipped over my hand and saw the deep cut, which was so clean I didn't even feel it at first! I scrambled downstairs to grab paper towels, pressing them to the wound, but it bled so much that each one became instantly saturated with blood. I couldn't replace the paper towels fast enough! I started to feel a little woozy, and that's when I knew I was in trouble.

Panic set in. I wondered, *Do I call an ambulance or do I call my parents a couple miles up the road?* Frugal me decided to call my parents instead of paying for an ambulance ride. I figured they would be here in 10 minutes, tops. My dad answered, and he could immediately hear the fear crackling in my voice. I couldn't even hold the phone with my good hand for fear of taking pressure off my other hand and further opening the floodgates of my new wound.

Seven. Eight. Nine minutes went by. *My dad should be here any minute, I kept thinking.* Ten minutes, and no sign of his silver Toyota Corolla. I blasted through the remaining paper towels, and began to worry about passing out. I called my dad again to see where the heck he was at. Turns out he was waiting for my mom to get ready (Insert face palm emoji here). I urged him to hurry up.

After what seemed like an eternity, we finally arrived at the hospital. I jumped out of the car and ran through the emergency room doors. The secretary didn't even look up to greet me. She asked my name, insurance, and all that business. Finally she looked up and saw the pool of blood that had collected on my new paper towel. She flew up out of her chair to call over another employee, who escorted me to a room right away.

The doctor finally arrived. He took one look and told me to thank my lucky stars I didn't slice through any of my tendons. He jabbed a needle into my injured hand to pump in some novocaine. After waiting for a few minutes with the nurse he came back in, ready to insert the stitches. He sewed the first suture to start tying my flap of skin back to the rest of my hand. After the second one went through he noticed I was grimacing in pain.

He asked, "Can you feel this?"

"Oh, yes," I said. The novocaine wasn't working.

"Do you want me to stop?" he asked.

"No," I groaned. "Just get it done."

Thirteen stitches later, there I was with a newly laced-up hand, minimal bleeding, and a few big lessons learned.

- Lesson #1: Confidence = Awesomeness. Cockiness = Humbling experience ahead.
- Lesson #2: You need the right tools and skills for the tough parts of the job.

A Puddle of Electricity

What I thought was going to be a two month bathroom reno project ended up turning into a year and a half. But I never gave up and finally got there. I had just finished installing the sink vanity. The shower wall was tiled, flooring installed, and walls erected, with no further injury to myself. All I had left to do was attach the hoses back to the hot and cold water spouts and turn the water back on. Then, voila! My bathroom reno would be complete!

I finagled my hands and wrench into the tiny space in the vanity. I cranked on the wrench a couple times to make sure the hoses were tightened. Seemed good to me. I can't tell you how proud I felt! I stood smiling in that bathroom with my chest puffed out and an imaginary cape flying off my back, fluttering in the proverbial breeze. I had done it!

I excitedly descended two flights of stairs to the basement, where the main water shut-off valve was. I grabbed the handle and turned the valve on. I rapidly climbed the first flight of stairs. Then I heard something. Dread set in as I sprinted up the second set of stairs to the top floor. *Oh, no.* Water was spraying everywhere! Both the hoses had unhooked and were whipping water around like crazy. I dove into the water fight and quickly caught hold of the two slithering snakes causing all the damage. I aimed their gushing streams toward the tub.

My clothes were drenched. I shed my soaking shirt and pants and scooted back down the two flights of stairs to the main water valve shut-off. Phew! Disaster somewhat averted. I now know I should have used the local shutoff valves, but you know what they say about hindsight...

I trudged upstairs to the first floor. *Drip...Drip...Drip.* I peered into the downstairs bathroom. Beads of water were jumping off the ceiling light fixture and falling to the floor. *Shoot!* I grabbed a bucket out of the closet.

I scurried back upstairs. My newly renovated bathroom looked like it had gone through the washing machine. I put a fan on, hoping to accelerate the drying process.

I dipped back downstairs to check on the first floor bathroom. The bucket collected a fair amount of water. I decided to check the basement laundry room (right below my downstairs bathroom) for good measure. I turned the corner, flicked the light on, and—*splash!* My bare foot stepped right into a puddle. I heard the ever familiar *drip...drip...drip.* I turned to see the water landing right on top of an active plug.

Afraid an electrical fire was going to start, I knew I had to react fast. *Should I take the plug out? I wondered.* I inspected the plug quickly, decided it was plastic, and reached forward to pluck it out of the socket with the tips of my thumb and index finger.

On contact I knew I had made what could have been a fatal mistake. My fingertips immediately felt the cool, smooth metal of the old plug. Electricity. Metal. Water. Me standing in a puddle. I was a math teacher at the time, but I didn't need to be to know that those elements were an equation for disaster. I was instantly lit up like a Christmas tree. I could feel the volts of electricity running through my body. I even had a little black smudge mark where it exited my body.

I stood there absolutely stunned. I examined my hands and feet. Everything was in tact. My body felt a little weird, but I was alive! What I had thought was going to be a celebratory day—and the end of my hard work—turned out to be a disaster, but in that moment I was so grateful to be alive.

Lessons learned:

- Sometimes when you think you have finished or mastered something, life is going to continue to refine you and let you know you're not done just yet!
- Reach for the stars. Never a wet, metal plug!

PART 2 RECAP:
THE GPS TO LIFE'S ZEST

The truth is, we all get lost at some time or another, sometimes so much that we can't even find ourselves. This typically shows in our lives as angst and misery. Hurt or hatred. Fear or anger. We need to constantly return to finding ourselves, and continually come back to the GPS to find life's zest.

1. **G**ratitude
   - Focus on what you do have, not on what you don't have
   - Give yourself an experience that moves you

2. **P**resent
   - Set intention at the beginning of each day
   - Turn down the noise
   - Enjoy your burger (Take in a moment with all of your senses)
   - Find your own clouds (Connect with nature)

3. **S**ervice
   - Check who you are serving (Throw up the red flag if it's always yourself!)
   - Find the person, group, or cause you are passionate about
   - Take a look at your vision

- Identify what skills you have and need to best serve
- Connect with others for positive momentum

Now that we know where we are going with the GPS to Life's Zest, we need to head to the next section of our journey which covers the vehicles (Relationships) that are going to take us where we want to go!

PART THREE

RELATIONSHIPS

CHAPTER 12

JUMPING INTO CROC-INFESTED WATERS (LITERALLY)

I t was three-quarters of the way through my first year of teaching. A couple of my colleagues asked me to head down to Florida with them and their families during our April break. One of their in-laws had a house down near Bokeelia, Florida, located on the Gulf Coast side of the state. I had just landed at the airport in Fort Myers, where my buddies came and picked me up. We coasted down to the quiet little town, passing swaying palm trees and glistening bodies of water. Just what I needed for some quality relaxation time.

After a couple of days next to the in-ground pool, we woke up feeling adventurous. A canal ran along the back of the property. I was lounging in a chair and I heard my buddy's brother, Eddy, call out, "Nash, I dare you to jump into the canal!"

I laughed and said, "Only if you go first!" On any given day you could see a crocodile floating down the canal. Much to my chagrin, Eddy glanced over at our oldest friend and responded, "Okay. Pete, you in?" Pete responded with a hesitant, "Fiiiine." My other buddy Gary, who had invited me down and was by far the most jacked out of all of us, jumped out of his chair and begged us not to do it. He said we were crazy and that it was the dumbest idea ever. We shrugged it off and piled our way onto the dock.

Now put yourself into this situation. There are three of us. We are all going to jump off the furthest end of the dock and then swim about 20 feet in croc-infested waters to the other side. Would you rather go first, second, or third? Well, I certainly didn't want to be the last one! By that time the croc underneath the dock would figure out we were serving up free meat that day. I didn't really want to be the first one either, just in case there was a ravenous monster lurking below. I figured the second spot was the safest. All three of us peered down into the water. You couldn't see the bottom. We would never have admitted it, but all three of us were starting to tremble from nerves.

Without warning, Eddy jumped in! He figured he didn't want to be the last so he may as well be the first. The two of us remaining were startled. He poked his head out of the water, motored over to the far edge of the dock to where there should have been a ladder, and pulled himself up. He smiled; he knew he made it. As he climbed back out of the water we realized he was bleeding. He scraped his leg on the dock. Awesome. Fresh blood in the water. Nothing like adding blood to a feeding frenzy.

Suddenly, Pete courageously took a giant leap off the dock! There was no way he was going to be the third one in. He frantically swam over to the other side of the dock. He quickly pulled himself up and tried to catch his breath. He announced, " I made it! Nash, it's your turn!"

I can't back out now, I thought. (Absolutely I could have backed out now!) I scanned the top of the water. No movement. From the safety of the lawn Gary yelled, "Nash, don't do it!" But it was too late. My feet left the dock and I landed in the water with a big splash. Thirty seconds of pure adrenaline. My hands were voraciously churning up water. My heart was pounding. It seemed to last for eternity. But I finally touched the other side of the dock! Phew!

It couldn't have been more than a minute after our celebratory high-fives on the dock that Pete yelled out in panic, "My wedding ring! It came off!" His wife, boiling over with anger, screamed back, "Are you kidding me?" Her icy stare was enough to make everyone feel uncomfortable. We ran over to the dock to see if we could catch a glimpse of anything shiny resting on the muddy floor below. We couldn't see a darn thing. *He is so screwed,* I thought to myself.

For the next hour it was pretty silent. We just basked in the rising sun, pointedly not acknowledging the chaos that just happened moments before. Pete refused to leave the dock. He laid down on his belly and peered endlessly into the waters below. Poor guy. He was devastated. I'm not sure how long he sat there, but suddenly he sprang up off the wooden planks and exclaimed, "I see it!" We rushed over in disbelief. Sure enough, the waters had settled and there was a bright, shiny object throwing out reflections from the bottom of the canal floor! What a lucky son of a gun!

We quickly realized there was one massive problem. We were up here and the ring was down there in the dangerous abyss below. Pete didn't want to move from his post. He had a laser-like focus on the ring and wasn't going to chance losing sight of it. He didn't want to just dive in and go for it. That would stir up the muddy waters and risked dislodging the ring. We might never see it again. That's when Pete had the audacity to tell us that someone else was going to need to go in slowly from the shore and retrieve it. *No way,* was my first thought. Navigating croc-infested waters and moving slowly should never be put in a sentence together. While Pete kept an eye on his ring from the dock, the rest of us were back on shore trying to talk out the scenario. We quickly realized there was only one of us that was single at the time and didn't have any kids, and we decided that was the best person for the job.

And guess who that poor sucker was?

I was about to tread through some pretty dangerous waters. *Again.*

No one could believe I was doing this. *I* couldn't believe I was doing this. There I was, knee deep in the warm, dark waters of the canal. I was about 10 yards from the prized possession, and all the *National Geographic* replays of crocodile attacks were running through my thoughts. My fear was so tangible you could have cut it with a knife. Pete had his eyes locked on the ring below. Eddy and Gary were nervously on the lookout for any movement. I knew how fast and powerful crocs could be. If there was one that wanted me I was a goner (Can my mom and dad still punish me in my thirties? The first time they read this they are going to have a conniption).

My feet sunk into the mud as I managed to summon the courage to slowly shuffle forward. I had to be cautious not to disturb the muddy bottom. The water touched the bottom of my bathing suit. My instincts were screaming at me to abort this mission, but I continued to slowly trudge on. I could hear encouragement from the shore,

"Nash you got this!"

And then, all of a sudden, I could see it. Straight ahead of me. It was staring right back at me. The ring, that is.

The water was about to crest over my head. *I'm going to have to dive underwater to pick it up,* I realized. I held my breath and dove. Underwater, I opened my eyes to see the shiny ring on the floor. Fear at this point is boiling in my veins. I frantically grabbed for the tiny circle, but my fear got the better of me. I rushed it, and my hands closed around nothing but silt. I came up empty-handed, but I grabbed a quick breath of air and rushed right back down to feel around for it again. By this point, the water was getting murky again. I couldn't feel the ring and Pete could no longer see it. I retreated from the water and scrambled in shame to the shore.

Twenty minutes ticked by as we waited for the muddy waters to settle once again. By this point, the sun was at its strongest. Beads of sweat were dripping down my face. For a second time, my buddy shouted, "I can see it!" My jaw dropped, and we rushed over to take another look. Sure enough, the ring was sitting there half-uncovered on the floor below. Gary said, "Nash, there is no way you are going in a third time. This is insane!"

Too late.

I was already heading into the water. This time, I moved quicker. I wanted this over and done with. I could feel my heart rate and breathing start to increase as I waded out to the ring in half the time it had taken me on my first go. I was practically standing on the ring. I knew I had one shot at this and had to get it right. I took a quick breath and dove to the bottom. I took my right index finger and placed it right through the circular ring.

There was no way I was letting this out of my grip. I pushed off the soft, muddy bottom, and broke the surface of the water. As if I had just won a national championship I had the ring positioned on my index finger showing everyone we were #1. Cheers erupted!

For the first couple of years after that trip, Pete texted me and thanked me on his anniversary of his marriage. He gave me huge kudos and explained to me that I was a large part of the reason they were still married. I was glad I was alive to text him back.

Why did I tell you this story? It is the perfect example to help us define relationships. Think about all your relationships with friends, family, teachers, and strangers. How many times have you felt the need to jump into a situation you don't feel comfortable with? Half the time you know it is as dangerous as navigating croc-infested waters, but you go along with it anyway. Relationships take place in muddy waters. Often times it's hard to see or predict what is lurking underneath. How do you navigate them successfully? Relationships can be super rewarding but carry with them a lot of risk. Some relationships will fail. We enter back into the waters even though we know its dangerous. We need them to survive and thrive. Let's take the plunge into the next chapter in learning how to deal with the authorities in our lives.

Disclaimer: Do not jump into actual waters infested with crocodiles. We will talk about decision-making in this chapter. Jumping in (three times) was stupid. When I was younger I thought I was invincible. Looking back at this now, I never would have done it again. I could have robbed so many people of so many things. The truth is, your life matters way more than you know.

CHAPTER 13

DEALING WITH THE AUTHORITIES

I magine you're just driving along, minding your business, and then somewhere behind you these blue lights start flashing. You immediately think *Are they pulling me over? Did I do something wrong?* The flashing lights get brighter and brighter and that pit in your stomach gets bigger and bigger. You are praying the officer drives right past you (If you don't drive yet, watch your parent's or older brother's reaction next time it happens). This anxiety happens in almost all of us.

As teens we have a similar reaction when a teacher or parent comes after us. We get that feeling in our stomach, and we might even lash out or dismiss whatever they are charging us with. Why do we do that? Why do adults have to bother us with such petty things?

Decision-Making: Teens vs. Adults

The truth is, teens and adults think differently. They literally use different parts of their brains for decision-making. My high school psych teacher used to tell me I didn't use my prefrontal cortex to make a decision. Turns out he was right. The year after I graduated college, *Harvard Magazine* released an issue with an article by Debra Bradley Ruder called *The Teen Brain*. In the article it discusses that only 80% of your brain is developed during your teenage years, and that it isn't fully developed until around age 25! The prefrontal cortex is responsible for decision-making, planning, judgement, and all that good stuff. Yours isn't fully developed yet. So where does your brain go to make these decisions? The amygdala. The amygdala is the part of your brain that controls your emotions. At your age, you are more wired to make a decision based off your emotions rather than logical processing and known information. But here's the good news: simply knowing this information about your brain is a massive strength. You need to take your time with your decisions and ask yourself, "Am I making this decision based on my emotions or because I actually think it is the right choice?" Most of the time when you react to something your parents said and turn into an angry, cornered wolverine, you may be making an emotional decision (I'm just saying). Take your time with your decisions.

A lot of adults don't know this information about your brain, either. They don't get why you can get A's in school but then make a poor decision while hanging with your friends. Tell your parents, guardians, and coach about this. This is not to create an excuse. You don't get to blame a poor decision on this newfound information. Instead, use it to empower you and the adults in your life by letting them know that you may need some patience and understanding as you go through this time in your life.

Why Your Parents and Guardians Are All over Your Tail Feather

Despite what you may think, I have found the vast majority of nagging parents have good intentions. I can't say they all have the most productive approach of communicating this with you, but the good intent is there. Your parents don't want you to feel pain. They don't want you to make the same mistakes they did at your age. Most of them don't want to watch you struggle. They want to watch you succeed, smile, and be happy. It's hard for some of them to see that your struggles are necessary, and that they will help you to succeed in the end game.

Parents and guardians do have one thing typically on their side which you most likely don't: experience. They have been in your shoes. Sure, not your exact ones, but maybe the same brand. They may have struggled in school, been through some tough relationships, had some awesome times with their friends, or struggled to make them. Despite what you might think, your parents actually may be able to relate to your circumstances. Who knows, they may even have some solid advice for you. Some parents aren't too great at explaining and relaying their experiences with you. This is why "learning conversations" are so important, as you learned in the first part of the book. You're pretty smart and I bet your parents are, too. If you can learn to have open conversations with one another and have the patience to listen to each other, I can almost guarantee all your lives are going to get a little bit easier.

At the end of the day your parents or guardians are responsible for you. You didn't come with instructions. They are figuring it out just like you are. Many adults tie their own identity to that of their children. They don't want to be seen as a failure just like you don't. You both need to flip your mindsets and understand you are all on the same team. You need to understand challenges are going to come up. Embrace those challenges, because they are there to help you both grow.

How To Win Adults Over

Step 1: Use more than one word.

I am going to go out on a limb here. When you come home from school and your mom asks you how was school today, you probably say some version of good, fine, boring, etc. She may follow up and say, "Anything happen?" and of course you always say, "Nope." Followed by you walking into another room.

You've just missed a golden opportunity. You could have invested three minutes and received enormous gains later. Humans get into routines, and this includes you and your parents. When your parent asks you about school, they are trying to relate to you. They want to know that you're doing well or even when you're not doing well. They need and want feedback. I get it. You just had a long day of school and you don't have it in you to listen. So talk. Tell them something exciting that happened. Tell them about your ideas for your chemistry project, or how you contributed to the class discussion during English. Most of your parents aren't good at asking the right questions to get you talking (I'm thinking this might be my next book). Next time you get home from school, talk to them about something that excites you. If your parent is a talker or an interrupter, start the conversation with, "Hey Mom, I've got something to share but really just want you to listen while I tell it if that's okay?" I've seen this work over and over with developing better relationships for teens. It's quick. It's productive. It opens up the communication lines. Your parents will feel connected to you, and they are going to trust you more and more when they know what is going on inside that noggin of yours.

Step 2: Earn trust by doing the little things.

I'm going to tell you a little story. My older sister, Erin, may or may not kill me for sharing it, but it's a risk I'm going to take. When she was a teen, adults loved Erin, but she proved to be human like the rest of us. Late one night when I was about fourteen, my dad got a phone call. A group of high schoolers had just been busted for drinking in the woods, and my sister Erin was one of them.

As you know, choices have consequences. Erin was grounded, and rightfully so. She broke the law and was lucky she wasn't arrested. My dad was furious with her, and he made it clear that she had broken his trust.

Erin quickly demonstrated that she knew the formula for working with adults. You need to do the little things right before they are going to trust you with the big things. A day or two later, I heard the buzzing of the lawnmower. *Wait a minute, I thought, confused.* My dad wasn't home and I was inside. *Who is running this thing?* I peered out the window and there was Erin, walking behind our John Deere push-mower. I smirked, thinking to myself, *This is going to be awesome.*

Sure enough, fifteen minutes later I could hear Erin scream-ing my name. I scrambled outside, worried about the carnage I was about to see, but when I saw the damage, I couldn't help but chuckle. She ran over my dad's new hose. *He's going to be pissed,* I thought. *This is epic.* My dad will deny this, but he's definitely always had a soft spot for Erin, and she was finally at the bottom of his list.

Now let's all learn from Erin's mistake and her approach to fixing it. Like I said before, adults loved Erin. Coaches, teach-ers, parents, our parents—everyone thought she was the best. She was an expert at doing the little things that were asked of her but also the ones that weren't. She went out of her way to make herself useful, and adults trusted her as a result. But with one big, bad decision, she lost some of that trust, and getting it back wasn't an easy task. Even after the lawn mowing incident she persevered and didn't deter from her approach with adults. She did the little things, and with each extra chore and kind act, my parents began to trust her more and more. Slowly but surely, Erin earned back her privileges. Parents understand that one choice could mess up your entire life; they may even know someone who still deals with the consequences of a choice they made in their teenage years. Typically as teens, we don't think that far ahead, but the truth is that one drink, one post, or one choice absolutely can equal GAME OVER. Show the adults in your life you can make good decisions with the small things, then you will have better conversations when you ask them for the big things.

The One Adult You Need in Your Life

A high school soccer team went up to a camp in Maine to bond and get in some quality training before their first game of the season. Fast forward four days in, when one of the junior boys is pounding on a sophomore who just went hard into a tackle. It's a complete overreaction from the junior, a super angry kid that could get pissed off easily. He had a lot of darkness inside. Off the field he seemed like a super nice kid. A little quiet maybe, but not this angry jerk he was on the field.

Insert Mr. Carson, the varsity coach. Later that night, he pulled this angry junior aside while the rest of the team was hanging out. They sat down at an old, weathered picnic table. The player knew he had stepped over the line. He knew this conversation was coming. Any coach would have had the right to read him the riot act or kick him off the team. But Mr. Carson wasn't any coach; he took the conversation in a different direction.

"I can tell something is really bothering you," said Mr. Carson. "What's going on?"

The player was thrown off-guard. He took a second to think about it, and responded, "Nothing."

Mr. Carson clearly didn't believe him, and continued, "What I saw out on that field today isn't you. Are you sure something isn't up?"

The angry junior could feel his eyes starting to get glassy, and he struggled to hold back tears. "Yup," he said shortly.

Mr. Carson nodded. "Alright then. I'm here for you. Anytime you need to talk about anything."

It was a conversation that changed that high school junior's life, though he never told Mr. Carson that, and I can say it with certainty because that angry young soccer player was me. If I could go back and do it all over again, I would have opened up and told him everything. At the time, I knew that if I did, I was going to bawl my eyes out and I felt like he would have seen me as weaker. I know now that he would have seen it as courageous. The truth is, I was going through hell. I hit rock bottom and knew I was depressed. I just didn't know what to do about it. Yeah, Mr. Carson had every right to ream me out, but instead he decided to change my life. He gave me the one thing I needed in my life: a trusted adult I could talk to.

They Help You Navigate Difficult Situations

Back when I was teaching I had a student named Allan. Allan was known for being a class clown, and he was a fairly popular student both in and out of school. One day before class he approached me and asked if we could talk.

"I have this friend," he started, and immediately it clicked in my mind—*okay, so this friend is you.* I told myself to keep an open mind. Allan continued to tell me that this "friend" brought something his parents didn't want in the house, and he was worried his "friend's" parents knew about it. "What should I do?" he asked me.

I asked if this was his friend's choice to bring this to the house. He assured me it was. I told him, "Your friend has to own his decision. Every choice has a consequence, positive or negative. Lying only gets you further from the truth and in more hot water."

I told him to make sure to tell his friend that he needed to come clean with his parents. He needed to make it clear that he made a bad decision but also to follow up with why he did it. He should expect his parents to be upset but hopefully his honesty should earn him points in the situation. His friend needed to work with his parents to figure out how to ensure that this ill-advised decision would not happen again.

They Help You Reconsider Terrible Ideas

I don't think I realized every student needs a Mr. Carson in their life until I met a student who wanted to get a tattoo of my face on his buttocks. For this story we will call him Jack. Jack's dad was absent from his life. He was in a constant battle with his mom because of his choices, and he had a knack for driving adults insane. He tried his usual antics with me in my class, trying to rub me the wrong way. I quickly shared with him that I had worked with plenty of students who had been kicked out of schools for this or that. I told him they were some of the most loyal students I ever had after I earned their trust. I let him know I never gave up on a single one, even if they did threaten to kill me a few times. He appreciated this story, and soon his behavior changed. He let me know when he was struggling and with what. He loved that I came from the finance world and he would tell me these grandiose stories about what our business ventures would look like together. As the end of the year approached, he wanted to show me his gratitude for my sage advice and being there for him whenever he needed it. Most students would wait to make the present a surprise and give it to the teacher on the last day, but Jack wasn't most students.

I am unconditionally grateful this student decided to blurt his idea out in class in the last weeks of school. To describe Jack as impulsive would be an understatement—when he got an idea in his head, he would usually just do it, no questions asked. On this particular day, class had just wrapped up and we had about a minute at the end of class before the bell rang.

"Mr. Nash," Jack said, still in his seat. "I finally figured out what I am going to do for you."

I smiled. "All your hard work is enough for me, Jack. No need to get me anything."

"No, I'm getting you something," said Jack, with a huge grin on his face and a mischievous look in his eye that I knew well by this point. "You want to know what it is?"

"Sounds like you would like to share it." Hesitantly, I asked, "What is it?"

Jack said, "I'm going to get a tattoo of your face on my butt cheek."

Immediately, I felt shocked and slightly panicked, but I forced myself to remain calm as I told him, "While I am honored, please don't do that, Jack. Tattoos are permanent and you will regret that."

"I know they're permanent," said Jack with a shrug. "That's why I picked my butt cheek. No one is going to see it, but I'll always have you with me."

Ultimately, with more follow-up conversations I convinced Jack to absolutely not move forward with the tattoo. But what this conversation did show me is just how much me investing my time and being there for Jack meant to him. I was his Mr. Carson.

Every one of you needs a trusted adult like this in your life. Typically at your age this may be someone who is not one of your parents. Things can get awkward talking to your parents about certain things, so you lean on people outside of your family. Whether you have one already or not, you need an adult in your life that you know will always be there for you through the ups and downs.

Trusted adults come in all different forms:

- Teacher
- Coach
- Guidance Counselor
- Club Advisor
- Youth Group Leader
- Aunt or Uncle
- An older adult sibling
- YMCA staff member
- Therapist
- A friend's parent

But adults aren't the only people you need in your life in order to rock it. You also need the support of your peers.

CHAPTER 14

HIGH PEER PRESSURE

Your peers are honestly the group that has the most influence over you. You care about their feedback, solicited or not. They are your age, and live in your social atmosphere. They can build you up or tear you down. You can link with them to change someone's life in an incredible way or to destroy another's self-esteem. This group has power over you. Or do they?

Sweet 16 to the Elite 8

It was 2004, and I was a sophomore in college. We had just celebrated our 2-0 NCAA first round victory against a team from New York. We were the first men's soccer team in school history to make it this far. It was surreal to watch our team advance in the infamous NCAA tournament bracket.

We had just checked into our hotel in Hoboken, New Jersey, where we had incredible views of the Hudson River and New York City. Across the way, three years before, the Twin Towers would have stood. We were hoping to make history in an uplifting way.

It was a cool, crisp day. Perfect for another match in November. Our goal was to reach the Sweet 16. We were one win shy. As we were warming up, there was no crowd and the home team seemed late to show up. We were ready to annihilate them.

But then the whistle blew. Hundreds of fans poured out of the nearby frat houses to fill the seats. The other team's fans were relentless. Turned out our opponent was pretty darn good. We gave it our all, but our journey came to an end on that November day.

We didn't end up reaching the round of 16 but what we did end up with were the Elite 8: A group of eight friends that became unbreakable. Since that day, we have celebrated victories and overcome hardships. We've pushed each other to be better dads, better husbands, better coaches, and better people. When one of us falls down there is always another one of us to pull that person back up. We choose each other day in and day out. At your age I never thought a group like this was possible.

The Freedom to Choose

You do have the power to choose who you listen to, who you are going to be influenced by, who you hang out with, who you say yes to, and who you say no to. Turns out these choices have a tremendous impact on your life—my advice to you is to choose wisely.

1. You are who you hang out with.

I'm not going to get into the facts and figures and weeds with you on this but I'm giving you a heads up: There is plenty of research to support this statement. If you don't like who you currently are, there is a good chance you need to shuffle up your friend group. This can be a big decision, but secretly you'll know if it is the right one. If I could give myself advice at your age it would be to pick a handful of people you trust. Ask them to let you know when they see you making a bad decision and give you a pat on the back when you are crushing it.

2. Your goal is to grow.

If you aren't growing you aren't happy. No one can achieve happiness while remaining stagnant. The happiest teens I've seen are the ones who are constantly looking to grow and discover new ways to be a better human. Pair up with friends who have healthy and positive habits. By this age, you should be able to figure out what is a positive habit and what really is a negative one. Friends who drag you down to their level or have no interest in growing are a tell-tale sign it's time to break off from them or at least limit your valuable time with them. It's going to take a courageous conversation but luckily you can go back to the first part of the book to figure out how best to have it. Let them know you are looking to other avenues to help yourself grow in whatever area it is that you choose. Label the habit that you can no longer take part in. It isn't going to be easy, and harsh words might be exchanged, but in the long run you will be better off. Who knows? Maybe they want to change too, but didn't have the courage to make the leap. Maybe you just found a buddy to take that leap with you.

Dealing with Negative Influences

It's a lot easier said than done, right?! Typically your gut sends up the red flag to your brain letting you know when something doesn't feel right. Then the pressure gets put on you (or at least you feel like it does) to make the wrong choice. Otherwise you go down the rabbit hole of all the rumors, stories, or comments that will be said about you. You don't want to risk your identity. I don't blame you; I didn't want to either. But what if there is a way you can keep your cool factor without giving up your values? Truth be told, there is. We just spoke about cutting the negative peers out of your life. The question is, what do you do in the heat of the moment? What happens when you are presented with that tough decision and you're between a rock and a hard place?

Let's start with something on the simpler side: rumors. Rumors are just that, right? No big deal. No harm, no foul? Far from it. Rumors are self-esteem crushers. They're what cause some of you not to want to go to school. Ever. Again. None of us likes a rumor. Well, at least when it is about us. Let me ask you this question: How many rumors have you spread during the past week? What about the past month? Or the past year? Lost track? The solution to rumors starts with you. Make the choice now to stop spreading them. I'm not asking you to stand up to everyone and stop them. I'm asking you simply not to spread them. If everyone in your school made this one decision, it's crazy the change you would see. It's a bold request, but I challenge you to do it. Next rumor you hear, don't spread it. Most of the time they're not even true. Think about if you were on the other end of the rumor. Would you want it spread? You can control one person—yourself. Make the choice now.

Next up: What to do when you are presented with the choice to use drugs or alcohol. I'm not going to beat you to death with the negative effects or why you shouldn't do them. I'm sure you've already heard the spiel a number of times. What I am going to do is remind you that your brain isn't fully developed yet. Right now, your brain is wired to submit to risky behavior. Drugs and alcohol bring just that. Risk. Excitement. But your brain isn't wired to think of the aftermath of drugs or alcohol.

Poor decisions. Addiction. Possibly even death. Remember that next time you are presented with the choice to consume drugs or alcohol. I challenge you to make the healthy decision to stay clear of these negative influences.

Okay, so let's go to a hypothetical here because if I'm going to challenge you I need to at least give you some of the tools to be successful. Let's say you show up at a party at Jason's house. You were pretty sure Jason never drank and were kind of sure his parents were going to be there, so you told your parents there was going to be no drinking. But then you get there and Jenny shows up with her older brother, who brings two handles of vodka. Jason takes out a red Solo cup and gives one to you. He pours some cranberry juice in your cup. You start to sweat, knowing what is coming next. Jenny's older brother is making his way over to you. With the handle. *Oh crap. What do I do?*

The answer is simple, with a huge side of courage.

"Hold out your cup," says the older brother.

"No thanks," you reply. "I'm all set. Thank you, though."

Jenny's older brother rolls his eyes. "C'mon. I'll just pour a little bit. Don't be a tightwad."

You smile at him. "No, really. I'm all set. I don't drink. Thanks for respecting that."

"Fine. Enjoy your cranberry juice." He sighs and moves on to the next person.

I have witnessed this conversation dozens and dozens of times. I was you. I never drank in high school. The first few times were hard, but I stuck to my guns. Eventually it became a habit, and soon it was a known entity. And despite always thinking everyone was going to call me a loser, they didn't. Sure, they gave me a hard time sometimes, but nothing over the top. They actually ended up respecting me for it. Eventually, my peers were the ones answering the question for me. "Nash doesn't drink," they would say, before anyone had even offered me alcohol. I still was invited to parties. I chose to attend the ones without alcohol and drugs. And if anyone tried to force it upon me, I didn't give them the time of day. The Centers for Disease Control and Prevention released a study that stated approximately 33% of high school aged students consumed a drink in the past month. That means two out of three of you don't drink. Keep that in mind. There seems to be a story we tell ourselves at your age that everyone is doing it, but that's all it is—a story. Not the truth.

Next topic: Addiction. It typically involves a very negative connotation. Let's define it as something we do or get repeatedly to feel a certain way, even when we know it's not good for us. Some of us are addicted to being popular and will do anything to get there. Some of us are addicted to fame. Some to money. Shopping. Pornography. Alcohol. Drugs. Addiction is crippling. Maybe it makes you feel good for a little bit, but the high of getting your fix wears off faster and faster, leaving you feeling awful. It can take over your life, change your personality, alienate friends, or tear apart families.

If you know you are addicted there is only one action that I've ever seen help: You need to tell somebody. You need to own it and find a professional to help deal with it. Most people hide their addiction until it's too late. If you know you are addicted or worry you are developing an addiction, you need to tell someone. ASAP. Addiction doesn't make you a horrible person and it doesn't define who you are. Know that going into this. You cannot do this alone. If you don't want to tell someone you know, there are anonymous hotlines you can call in your state or even people you can talk to online. Your life will almost always be handicapped if you don't handle this right now.

CHAPTER 15

THE PIRANHA IN OUR LIVING ROOM

All of a sudden, I heard my wife, Tara, let out a high-pitched scream. I peered into the living room to see Tara straddling the plastic safety gates we had just put up in the doorways. She started shouting, "I can't do this anymore! We literally have a piranha in our living room! I can't even live in my own house!" I smirked and let out an ill-advised chuckle.

We definitely did have a piranha on our hands, but this piranha had a thin, tan coat, and a cute little black and white mug paired with some razor-sharp puppy teeth. Tara was talking about Sedona, our three-month old rescue pup from Alabama. Tara had never raised a dog before and Sedona was fully demonstrating what the teething phase looked like.

A few weeks later we had our first visitor, Ross, my brother-in-law. He is about 5'8", and extremely skinny, weighing in probably around 125 pounds. Definitely not the most intimidating man you've ever seen. Ross cracked open the back door and announced his presence. I immediately expected Sedona to sprint over and jump on him. I was so ready to practice what we had been working on in our training classes, the ever powerful command, "Off." So was she going to listen to me or not?

I was shocked by what I witnessed next. Sedona ran in the opposite direction of Ross and cowered in the corner. Our fun-loving, kissing and hugging, no worries pup was scared stiff. Ross went over and tried to let her sniff the back of his hand but Sedona was startled and wouldn't let him get close enough.

These two stories are absolutely perfect in portraying what it can be like to be in any relationship. This cute, attractive, cuddly little puppy—your relationship—can be painful and upsetting if not taken care of correctly. Luckily, I've got some tools to share with you that will help you rock your relationships, new or old.

Just like with difficult conversations, relationships can trigger our own mini heart attack. I've found that CPR is not only the best method for helping us with difficult conversations but also for achieving and maintaining healthy relationships.

Communication
P
R

"Communication works for those who work at it."

—John Powell

Ask anyone in a long-term happy relationship and most people will tell you that communication is the key to their success and happiness. I can't say I disagree. If we go back to Tara and Sedona, the issue of communication in their relationship rears its ugly head. First off, they speak two different languages, which is the case with most partners in a relationship (And yes I'm including humans here!). Tara is speaking English to Sedona ("Don't eat my shirt."), which Sedona doesn't understand yet. Sedona is screaming at Tara that her gums hurt because of her newly acquired teeth. How would Tara know that? Tara then decides to yell louder and Sedona decides to chomp more, each hoping the other one will finally understand. Eventually the frustration between the two boils over. If these two are going to have a happy and loving relationship they are going to need to learn to communicate with one another. Luckily we have the C's of Communication to help us to understand one another and speak a common language.

Confidence

I'm going to refer back to one of Maslow's Hierarchy of basic needs here: safety. We all need to feel safe, especially in relationships. You may be thinking, *But Pat, safety starts with an S!* Yes, that's true. So let me use a different word that I feel every relationship has to have in order to be successful TRUST (I know, also not a C). In my eyes no trust means no healthy, happy relationship. It's impossible. I'm sure you have heard this or even felt this before, but what is trust exactly?

For this book, trust is going to be defined as the **C**onfidence (ah yes, the C!) you have in someone, including yourself, to perform or not perform an action. Let's go back to the story with Sedona and Ross. When I come home from work every day Sedona greets me with a rapidly wagging tail. She gives me a kiss on the hand, and then flips onto her back for the irresistible belly scratch. When Ross entered the door, Sedona ran away and cowered. Why? She didn't not have confidence in Ross, YET. The truth is, we have no idea what happened in Sedona's past when we got her. Had a former owner struck her previously? Sedona was wary and I'm sure rightfully so in her mind. Sedona's lack of confidence in Ross was preventing a happy and healthy relationship from forming.

Twenty minutes after Ross entered our house he was sitting at the dining room table in the living room. Sedona finally decided to enter the room with a little wag of her tail to let us know she was doing alright. She locked eyes with Ross and zoned in on him. She nervously took a couple steps forward and then stopped. Her tail wagged a little more as she got closer. She finally grew confident enough to walk up and sniff him. He reached out to pet her and she jumped back, her tail going a million miles a minute. Sedona sized Ross up one more time, pulled in tight next to his leg and received the open hand to start their relationship. A trusting friendship was forming with the growth of Sedona's confidence in him. Confidence is key!

Clear Expectations

Tara, armed with her own newfound confidence from working with a professional dog trainer, discovered Sedona had no idea what Tara wanted or was saying. Often when there is an issue in a relationship, expectations are not being met and most of the time they have not been communicated *clearly.* Remember it is very rare that you and the partner in your relationship speak the same language. We all come from different families and backgrounds, and even if you understand their words, it's not a given that you are understanding the intent behind them. There is a reason I included the difficult conversation part of this book first. It taught you how to effectively communicate, which includes both LISTENING and EXPRESSING your thoughts. How do we make sure expectations are clear between two people (or a person and a dog)? We acknowledge what the other person said and repeat it back to them to make sure we both understand and agree. Make sure the other person does the same.

As soon as Tara and Sedona began communicating more clearly to one another, they began to move in the right direction. Now when Sedona started nipping and flashing those pearly whites, Tara knew Sedona's teeth and gums were bothering her. Tara established the expectation that she would give Sedona a toy to help soothe the pain but only when Sedona approached her calmly and sat. You should have seen how excited they were when they finally figured this out. Now it was Tara flashing her pearly whites while Sedona's tail was wagging along the ground a mile a minute.

With our communication locked down, let's add another ingredient to the mix. A little bit of sugar goes a long way in a successful relationship.

CHAPTER 16

WE ALL NEED SOME SUGAR IN OUR LIVES

A few years after college I wanted to keep my passion of playing soccer alive, so I joined a co-ed soccer league with some of my close friends. One night after a late game we decided to go across the street and grab a couple of pizzas. We were shooting the breeze for a bit when the crowd dwindled down to a few of us. The conversation had turned to serious dating relationships.

"Before you get married you need to go see a marriage counselor," said my friend, a woman we called Sugar. "It will be the best money you ever spent!" My mind was blown. I thought when you are about to get married you should already have an awesome relationship, hence why you are marrying them. I asked Sugar to explain her thinking. "Well think about it, Pat. You are taking two completely separate lives and putting them together. You don't think there's going to be any problems with that? The food you eat, the way you do laundry. Not to mention all the baggage each of you bring from your family and past relationships."

Sugar was an absolute straight-shooter. She didn't hide any of her thoughts behind any curtains. When she got an idea she went for it. Once, she even convinced me to buy a bike that cost over $1000, train with her twice, and then ride in a 175 mile charity ride in a matter of a week. I bonked, flipped over a set of train tracks, and rode that last 30 miles in one gear, but it was one of the most memorable moments in my life because of her zest for life. She had an incredible sense of humor and could always make you smile.

I really looked up to Sugar and her husband. They seemed to have a great relationship and solid family values. Her husband owned a successful business that he engineered after starting in the lowest position possible in the company. They exposed their children to helping less fortunate people across the world. I wanted what they had. A happy and healthy relationship. What allowed them to have this?

Communication
Problem Solve
R

"When solving problems, dig at the roots
instead of just hacking at the leaves."

—Anthony J. D'Angelo

Whether you're working on a school project, getting your parents to see eye-to-eye with you, or deciding what to do with your friends, you are bound at some point to run into a problem. The problem could be something as small as deciding where to go out to eat or something as big as needing to break off a relationship. Communication, coupled with your newly acquired difficult conversation skills, will be pivotal in helping you work through problems. Diagnosing the problem is not always as easy as it sounds especially if there are multiple contributing factors. Let's talk about the P's to Problem Solving in Relationships.

Preparation

What Sugar was really talking about when she brought up therapy was the idea that you need to prepare for your relationship. The more intimate and longer the relationship, the more important preparation will be. For example, if you are looking to get into a long-term relationship with someone you just met, you will need to do some prep work. If you just bumped into someone who was visiting from a foreign country that you'll probably never see again, there won't be too much prep work to do. So what does this prep work look like?

It's similar to laying the foundation of a new house. You typically don't just lay the foundation right on top of the ground. Instead you dig down deep with an excavator to remove the dirt, rocks, and debris from where your foundation is going to be poured. You then make sure it has the correct dimensions to hold your dream house.

Preparing for a meaningful relationship is the same way. Right now neither of you can see below the ground. You know there are rocks and debris down there but aren't sure where or how big. What are you going to do if you hit a boulder that you cannot seem to move? You need to have a plan for when problems arise. It could be that each of you agree to come together and discuss the best solution to the problem, or maybe you agree to sitting down with a neutral party to help you navigate a perceived pitfall.

Past Experiences

There is no one who knows your past better than you. Some of you have been burned pretty badly by someone you care about. Some of you have had tremendous support throughout each of the relationships in your life thus far. The truth is you all have dirt, pebbles, and boulders in your past. What you may not realize is that you carry this load of dirt, pebbles, and boulders around with you, which can have a major impact on a relationship. In the previous section about difficult conversations, we talked about your past triggers. Your boulders are often buried somewhere in this page. You may not be able to remove these boulders from your property but you don't want them to protrude into the walls of your foundation.

From past experiences you can also figure out what worked for you and what didn't. What were the things that drove you crazy? What did you enjoy? What upset you? What helped you trust that person? These are the types of questions you need to ask yourself before you get into a relationship.

CHAPTER 17

ADULTING

Three months after I graduated from college I landed my first real job that gave me my own health insurance and helped me contribute to a 401K. I worked in the finance department for a very well-known bank in Boston. I was doing adult things such as taking the train into work every day and wearing a suit and tie. I was finally going to be independent... even if I still did live at home with my parents.

My first day at work, I was in my small cubicle in an office full of other small cubicles, each filled with people ranging from my age to about fifty. Then there were the bosses. They had their own offices. My cubicle was right next to my boss's office. Next to his office was his boss. And next to him was the ultimate boss who had the corner office with a beautiful view of the city. Within an hour of being at my workplace, I heard my boss screaming and chewing out someone on the other line. Turned out to be his daughter. Not a great sign.

Fast forward six months. I HATED my job with a PASSION. I regretted coming to work every day. I was always the first one there and the last one to leave. I worked 12 hour days, all out of fear of my boss. Over those six months I had learned that there used to be three other people in my department but they all moved departments to get away from this man. They told me they were going to hire someone to help me, but that was four months ago.

Then it happened. The Ultimate Boss went to his underling boss, livid about some numbers. The underling boss then went to my boss and chewed him out. Then my boss came to me in a panic, sweat dripping down his face. Some numbers in one of our accounts were way off and everyone wanted to know where that money was. I'm talking hundreds of thousands of dollars!

A half hour later, I called my boss over. I let him know it wasn't showing up as a lump sum because it had been dispersed in varying amounts into different accounts. He immediately ran into his boss's office. He loudly proclaimed, "I found where the missing money went!" His boss smiled and they shook hands. My boss went back into his office like nothing ever happened. No acknowledgement, no pat on the back. All I ever got was yelling and screaming when something wasn't right. It wasn't the recognition I was looking for. It was another R word.

Communication
Problem Solve
Respect

"Respect is a two-way street, if you want
to get it, you've got to give it."

—R.G. Risch

I am a huge believer in the power of giving respect. Some of you may disagree with me here and I can understand that. Some of you may be in the camp of "I don't give respect until they earn it." But I am going to respectfully disagree with you here.

I have four Macintosh apples together in a see-through bag downstairs in my refrigerator. I bought two of them two weeks ago and another two about a week ago. I know the apples I bought two weeks ago are probably bruised and brown on the inside. The other two are most likely still fresh and perfectly ready to eat. Honestly, from the outside I can't tell the apples apart. I have no idea which ones are bruised and which ones are okay.

People are a lot like apples. They may present as all good on the outside but inside, they may be bruised. We have no idea of all the thoughts and experiences that make up another person. We can't see inside them. So what can we do if we are going to have a relationship with this person? My thought is to start off with respecting them. This is not the same as agreeing with everything they do or say. Treat them as you would want to be treated.

If you are getting stressed over a relationship and feel like you are having a mini-heart attack, come back and give yourself some CPR training. Is there a breakdown in communication? Do you need to do some more prep work in the area of problem solving? Are each of you giving each other respect?

Before we get into the ins and outs of your interactions with others, there is a more important relationship we need to tackle first. Let's see how we can perform CPR inside this relationship.

CHAPTER 18

YOUR MOST IMPORTANT RELATIONSHIP

There is one relationship that you spend more time with than any other. It can be absolutely beautiful and empowering. Your accomplishments can be immense when this relationship is healthy and vibrant. There will be periods when this relationship struggles and can be full of doubt. This is when negative thinking sets in and sabotage can take over. This relationship supersedes every other relationship because without it your other relationships honestly don't stand a chance. What is this relationship? It's your relationship with yourself!

Think about it. You constantly talk with yourself. Discussion goes back and forth about all different ideas, thoughts, and issues. It could be about what is going on in class, what's happening out on the basketball court or on stage at theater practice. You have emotions and feelings about yourself. Sometimes you feel so proud of what you have accomplished, but other times you hate something you said or did and wish you could take it back. More often than not, with a little self-care, you can grow this relationship into a happy and healthy one.

CPR in Action: Self

Communication

The biggest issue I constantly witness and at times experience myself is within the communication department. We have an innate fear about our identity being turned upside down. We let these fears seep into our bloodstream and poison our thoughts, ideas, and dreams. These beautiful ideas that could turn into something special and electrifying fizzle out, then are sent to die. We have to recognize when this is happening and reverse the process. We need to pump in the antidote and let the positive juices flow through our body. What we need is to have confidence in ourselves and our abilities. We need to have faith and trust in ourselves. Without this, you will be living your intended life at half capacity, not even close to the fullest.

Self-Confidence

During high school I was a pretty good soccer player. My name was commonly featured in our local paper about earning an assist or scoring a goal. After high school it was onto college and I started the year trying out for the soccer team. I have to admit my confidence in myself was really shaken. A lot of naysayers told me I wasn't good enough to play college ball. I was too small. Too weak. My touch wasn't good enough on the ball. There was just no way I would make the team.

It was a lot to block out the noise. I knew I had speed and a work ethic that would be hard for anyone else to match. I focused on these two things throughout tryouts. I let these assets shine and hoped and prayed I had enough to make the team. When the final cut roster went up outside the locker room I scrolled down the list—I couldn't find my name. My heart sank and my stomach turned over. A couple of the older guys were down by the locker room and started congratulating me. I looked back at the list. Whew! My name was on it!

I went on to have a great experience for my four years. I have to be honest though, I never played up to my ability. In high school I had this confidence in my ability that I could take on any other player offensively and defensively. I would make a positive contribution to my team at all levels. I did have great moments in college whether it be making a defensive stop, changing the momentum of the game with an assist, or scoring the go ahead goal. But often when I would receive the ball, I would get nervous and afraid to make a mistake. And when you start to think like that, that's usually when you end up making one.

I went on to coach high school soccer shortly after I graduated from college. It was then that I realized the power of confidence. My players were making the same mistakes as I once did, all because of their mindset. I began to focus on instilling confidence in them. I let them make this mistake in practice, demonstrated it wasn't a big deal, and then showed them they were capable of making the correct play. The team I took over had a couple wins in as many seasons. Five years later and we were division champs. I chalk most of those wins up to allowing my players to perform with confidence and a positive mindset that allowed them to continually get better.

Five Ways to Build Self-Confidence

1. Ask your family, friends, teachers, or coaches what you are good at or how you positively contribute.

2. When your mind goes into catastrophic thinking, challenge whether that is a thought you should really be listening to.

3. Try something. Fail at it. Learn from it. Try it again. Repeat. You will get better and more confident. Just remember my bathroom renovation story, and don't get *too* confident!

4. Visualize it. Whether it's something you want to accomplish or be a part of—if you can picture it, you can get there.

5. Positive self-talk. You know deep inside that you were meant to accomplish something awesome. Keep talking about how you're going to make the impact.

Problem Solve

Have you ever been in a situation in your life where you don't know what to do? You keep going back and forth with yourself on what's right or what's wrong. Do I do this, or do I do that? A lot of our decisions deal with these types of muddy waters. One of my favorite movies, *Shawshank Redemption*, has a main character—Andy Dufresne—who has to make a ton of important choices in his life after he is thrown in prison for a crime he didn't commit. At the risk of spoiling the movie, at the very end, a character describes him as "Andy Dufresne, the man who crawled through 500 yards of sh** and came out clean on the other side."

So how do we problem solve in poopy waters, make good choices, and come out clean on the other side (without having to go to prison)?

The answer: Core Values

You may have heard of Core Values before. I bet most of your schools have them. They could be posted in your main hall, on your school website, or in your handbook. At some point a group got together in your building and had to pick these core values. The question is why did your school need core values?

The truth is, most strong businesses and companies have core values as well. A leader in your school most likely recognized at some point the need for core values. There is one thing this leader realized is going to happen no matter what they do and that something is CHANGE. That's right. Things are going to change. Schools, businesses, and life in general are never static; they are always changing for good or for bad. So as a school or business they need to define how they are going to make important decisions amidst all these changes. The questions they ask include: who are we; what do we value the most; and what are the most important values we can lean on to make decisions?

Core Values are an absolute game changer. Whenever you are about to step into a hot mess, a decision is eating away at you, or you simply have no idea what to do, you always fall back to your core values to help make that decision. These core values are your light when you are having trouble seeing in the darkness. When you are lost and getting tossed about at sea and you are looking for land, Core Values are the lighthouse that lead you in the right direction.

When I was a freshman in college, one of my best friends, Quinny, used to always introduce me to someone I was meeting for the first time the same way. He'd say, "This is Nash, the nicest kid you'll ever meet." I'm not even sure he realized he did it. At first it drove me nuts. I was a freshman student-athlete trying to build some street cred among an older crowd. I wanted respect. Nothing like meeting a senior football player at a party and saying, "This is Nash. Feel free to step all over him because he is going to let you do it."

Truth be told, now I absolutely treasure those moments where Quinny spoke so highly of me. Not because of the recognition but because I can see the immense power of a core value. My core value of treating other people as I wanted to be treated was a pillar I fell back on then, and still do to this day.

But seriously, think about this power. You may not be in college yet or may not plan to attend college. It's an awesome, beautiful, chaotic, risky adventure. A freshman has newfound independence where s/he gets to make whatever decision s/he chooses. You are presented with so many different choices such as whether to attend classes that day, whether to drink or do drugs at parties, whether to treat the person you are on a date with respectfully or not. You've all seen movies displaying these choices and behaviors. The vast majority of us strive to be well-liked and fit in and maybe even to be popular.

Quinny was popular. Despite all the chaos and crazy "fun" everyone was having, Quinny always managed to point out how nice or good of a person I was. He was recognizing my core value. He was a witness to my decision-making process when I was put in various situations. Amongst all the noise and chaos, my light was shining through.

Time to Take Action: Identifying Your Core Values

- If a person who knew you described what type of a person you were, what would you want them to say about you?
- What are your non-negotiables no matter what happens to you in life?
- What type of actions would violate the very essence of who you are?
- Go back to an action in your life that filled you with regret. What core value did you violate that made you feel that way?

Use these questions to come up with your own list of core values. Here are a few examples to get you going:

- Treat every human being respectfully no matter their race, religion, appearance, or social status
- Family comes before anything else
- Honesty
- Commitment to hard work
- Reliability
- Loyalty to friends

A core value is at the heart of who you truly are. It's a pillar that holds up your life choices. Identify them now and it will make problem solving that much easier.

Respect

Do YOU respect yourself?

No, seriously. Take one minute before you read the next line and really ponder this question. Do YOU respect yourself?

I wish I could jump into your head right now. There are a lot of times where I would never want nor dare to jump into a teenager's thoughts, but at this one moment I wish I could. I'm serious, I really want to. If I could see your thoughts right now I could decipher whether you really truly respect yourself. Self-respect is at the very foundation and very core of every relationship including the one with yourself. Without self-respect it is virtually impossible to love yourself, and if you don't love yourself you impede your ability to give love to others. I firmly believe everyone needs and deserves to have the most loving relationships possible, especially with themselves. If you answered "Yes" to respecting yourself, that's great. Let's read through the rest of this section and see if there are areas where you can grow in self-respect. If you answered "No" to respecting yourself, I'm proud of your courage to acknowledge that. Now let's go ahead and fix it.

Chances are there is something you are struggling with right now. Something you haven't told anyone. It weighs you down like an anchor. Typically it's something that knocks us off course from something else we know we should be doing. Maybe you're an incredible songwriter but you haven't picked up a pen in weeks because you've been so down about your physical appearance. Maybe you've always been a great group facilitator at school but you don't participate anymore because you don't think you are smart enough. Maybe you stopped sharing your talents as a friend because you didn't think you were good enough for them anymore. I see it all the time. We allow ourselves to be unhappy or miserable because we feel trapped and don't even know how we ended up there.

Let's take an example. Beautiful people. Do me a favor: scroll through your social media and pick out five beautiful people you see. Now define beautiful people. When you're done come back to reading the rest of this section.

My guess is that if I looked over the majority of your shoulders you stopped on the girl with the killer smile that lights up a room, the guy with the striking blue eyes, or the cute girl that rocked that gorgeous semi-formal dress. You get the gist. What do all these people have in common? Something that is, in your opinion, physically attractive.

I asked you to define beautiful people and most of you went straight to looks. I'll admit this was a bit of a setup, but it's a trap we as humans fall into all the time. I'll tell you who can really identify all the beautiful people in a room: a baby. Yup that's right, a baby. Not the infant that was just born and won't go to anyone but their mother without crying. I'm talking a little bit older. There is a time in a baby's life where they will smile or reach out to literally anyone. It doesn't matter their sex, race, religion, sexuality, political views, etc. The baby literally interacts and shows affection to everyone. They haven't been taught or witness to any prejudice, bias, judgements, or preconceived ideas. They are willing to love anyone and expect the same in return.

So where am I going with this? We talked about how some of you are struggling with respecting yourself. There's something that you don't feel is beautiful about you, whether it's on the inside or out. You need to change this feeling if you are going to respect yourself. Let's keep going with the idea of physical beauty.

I see physical appearance as an issue with a lot of people your age. It's a dream crusher. A saboteur. Confidence killer. This may be hitting close to home and may be the thing causing you to lose self-respect. It could be that your hair isn't the right color, your nose is too big, or you feel as though you are overweight. You may think these thoughts on your own or someone may have made hurtful comments toward you. I constantly see people—not just teens—go straight to the "I'm Ugly" category. If this is you, then please remember the baby. I truly believe every person on this earth is beautiful in some form or another. Everyone has gifts and talents to offer. Sometimes the real beauty can be buried beneath years of hate, anger, or sorrow. But it's always there.

The first step you need to do right now is to forgive. Forgive yourself for allowing these thoughts to control you and define who you are. Forgive yourself for not being who you want to be or doing what you want to do. Forgive yourself for not being the best daughter or son, the best friend, the best person possible. Forgiveness is one of the most powerful gifts we can give ourselves. Take hold of those negative thoughts that have been holding you back. Close your eyes, see yourself taking those thoughts out of your head and place them into the imaginary box that is in front of you. Lock the box. Put the box on the shelf. Now open your eyes. Take a deep breath. You may feel the need to let out a good cry right now. You literally just locked up what has been holding you back from having an incredible relationship with yourself. You just jumped back on the road to becoming who you truly want to be.

The second step is to go to the mirror and focus on one or two things you like about yourself. It could be a physical characteristic, or maybe it's your creativity, your thoughtfulness, your voice, or your perseverance. You need to flip the table (Don't literally do this). We need to flip your mindset. So many people focus on one or two things they don't feel like they have and forget to focus on the things they do have. They forget the very things they possess that can contribute a lot of value to their own life as well as others. You need to focus on these things and work on accepting who you are right now with a caveat that you may want to change some things about yourself in the future. We need to accept that there isn't one person in the world who is perfect. We need to respect ourselves, our bodies, our gifts, and our intelligence, and realize that we each deserve respect from ourselves and others.

Alright I definitely went outside most of your comfort zones here. Let's rein it back in and get on to what most of you really care about: dating relationships.

CHAPTER 19

HEARTTHROBS AND HEARTACHES

Are you currently in a relationship with someone? Why did you get into this relationship? If you're not in one, do you want to be? Why or why not? These are all important questions to ask yourself. Relationships have the power to change your life. For better or worse. I want to help you spot those relationships that are going to set you up for personal growth. I'm not guaranteeing you won't have disappointments or hurt feelings or that everything is going to be hunkydory all the time. That's not realistic. What is realistic is finding someone that likes you for you. You can be who you really are in front of them and they will accept the real "you."

I'm speaking firsthand on this. It is so incredibly awesome to be with a person who accepts you for who you truly are. My wife, Tara, does just that. We are extremely different from one another. She likes to binge watch TV shows and I love to find a quiet place to read. She loves to go to a party with a group of friends and I love to take a walk alone with my dog in the woods. The point is, she embraces me for who I am even though I am different from her, and I do the same. Our differences actually help us to grow and understand one another.

I have to be honest though. There was a point when we were dating where we thought it was over. What saved the best thing that ever happened to either of us? We learned to have difficult conversations. We understood the importance of listening and getting out what was bothering us. We learned to problem solve issues in a way that was respectful. If you want to have an awesome relationship, you need to find an awesome person with aligned core values, and then master difficult conversations. If you can handle that, then you'll make a pretty unstoppable team. That's exactly how Tara and I feel now. We feel like we are unstoppable, and it's awesome!

You need to have an idea of who you are and who you want to continue to be. You need to come back to your core values. If you haven't decided what your core values are, you need to go back and do that now. I'm not saying these can't change but you need to have some strong core values to fall back to. You will quickly realize that if you don't recognize them and keep them in the forefront of your mind, then some situation, action, or conversation will point them out for you.

Let's say a core value of yours is treating people equally and fairly. Three weeks after you start dating your new boyfriend, he makes an off-hand racist joke. Up until this point you have had a great time with him and he has treated you with dignity and respect. What do you do? He has violated one of your core values.

You have at least three options:

1.   Say nothing and pretend like it never happened.

2. Break up with him (Immediately or after your date).
3. Have a difficult conversation to learn why he said that and if that is what he really feels. Also to let him know that treating people equally is one of your core values.

Most of you would choose 1 or 2 when put in the "live" situation, but if you want to really have a rewarding relationship, communication is key. You are two people from two different backgrounds, families, and mindsets. You now have the skills to have that difficult conversation and turn it into a learning conversation. You both may decide this relationship isn't for you. Better to find out now than a year down the road. You might also realize that he said it as a poor attempt to get you to laugh. Maybe your best friend is of that race and he is the one who told your boyfriend the joke. Your boyfriend took that as permission to use the joke outside of that context. Engaging in an actual discussion about it will allow you to learn about each other in a way neither of you would if you'd chosen options 1 or 2. Ultimately, you get to decide how you move forward with something like this.

*I will note that if someone is continually violating your core values, they are absolutely not for you. You won't grow and become a better person with them. Instead you'll struggle. The deeper you get into it the harder it typically is to get out.

It can also be helpful to label your core values up front for your partner. For instance, let's say one of your core values is that you believe sexual relations should take place only within marriage. You fear that because of this core value you are never going to find someone, or that once they find out about this core value they will break up with you. I'm going to ask you to lean into this fear. There is a reason you feel strongly about this. Don't change your core value for fear of something that hasn't even happened. I've actually seen the opposite to be true. People become more curious about your core value when they learn of it. Sure, some people are going to completely disagree with you and maybe even break it off with you over it. But that's absolutely okay. You found out that relationship was not right for you. Ultimately, you will find someone who respects your core values and truly respects you. This is a mutual point from which you can each grow moving forward.

Sometimes you'll find yourself in a situation where you know you need to say, "No." It could be a simple, "No, I'm all set, thank you," "No, I'm uncomfortable with that," or just a plain old "No, I'm not doing that." Maybe it's drinking alcohol, or going further sexually than you're comfortable with, or sneaking out at night. It could be something as trivial as your partner asking to copy your math homework so you two can spend more time together, but if you don't feel comfortable saying yes, your partner must respect that. If they do not, there should be a big red flag that goes up in that brain of yours. You need to be comfortable with walking away from this situation and this person. It's not an easy thing to do, but you'll have a gut feeling when you know you need to do it.

The Pitfalls of a Romantic Relationship

1. Jealousy

Jealousy is a natural feeling that I think almost every human has felt before. It's that feeling when you are a bit unsure of yourself, when you wonder if there might be something better than you out there.

Let me give you an example. It's a gorgeous, sunny afternoon and you are at a cookout with your girlfriend. You are hanging around, chatting it up in a circle of your mutual friends from school. Your girlfriend asks if you want another cheeseburger and you say, "Sure." She strolls the twenty feet to the table covered in grilled meat and condiments. She is grabbing your burger and is approached by an attractive guy a couple years older than you. He says something to her that makes her giggle, and your radar starts to go off. Your hair stands on your arms and suddenly your heart is beating fast with anxiety. She turns around and heads back to your circle. You play it cool like you didn't see anything. Secretly, this small interaction rocked one of your nerves...maybe you were a little jealous, we could say?

2. Fear

Fear is another completely natural feeling. What were you afraid of? Were you afraid this guy was going to steal your girlfriend? Or that your girlfriend would like him better than you? Do you feel confident in this relationship? In yourself? Have you had a negative experience before in this situation?

The question is how do you react in this situation? Do you make a side comment to your girlfriend? Do you approach that guy? What do you say to him? Or could that have just been a friendly interaction? Maybe your thoughts are just running wild? Fear isn't necessarily a bad thing. But if fear constantly controls your thoughts and actions, you might be making it tough for the people in your life to be in a relationship with you.

3. Control

Fear can quickly turn into control. Controlling yourself is good, but controlling your significant other or being controlled by your significant other is not so good. No one likes to be controlled.

Typically, controlling people are fearful or insecure about something, most likely themselves. Maybe they were burned in a past relationship. Maybe that's how they saw one of their parents interact with their significant other. If you feel like you are always trying to control a relationship, stop and wonder why that is? What are you insecure about, and what triggers those insecurities? Go back into the difficult conversations section and figure this out. You need to recognize and acknowledge what is going on before you can attempt to fix it.

When to Move On

Relationships are hard work. No matter who you are in a relationship with, you are bringing two different backgrounds, views, families, and personalities together. There is likely to be a clash at certain points. But when is it too much? When should you move on?

In my opinion, there are telltale signs you are heading down the wrong road with the wrong person.

Here are five signs it's time to get out of a relationship:

1. When the person won't let you hang out with your friends or family, or shows extreme jealousy when you do.

2. When the person physically, emotionally, or psychologically harms you.

3. When the person is constantly belittling you or showing disrespect.

4. When your trusted friends with your best interest at heart are telling you you've changed, and not for the better.

5. When the person is constantly lying to you or about you.

Relationships can be an awesome part of your life. Most likely you will go through a bunch and keep the ones that are right for you. During this time you will experience ups and downs. Just remember you deserve respect. If one relationship ends, there is another person out there for you down the road. When you are single, enjoy it and use the time to get to know yourself better. Do the things you love, hang out with friends, and keep an open mind.

CHAPTER 20

TO THE MOON AND BACK!

We had just hopped on a plane for another mission with the C.I.A. As we typically do on all our missions, we boarded wearing matching t-shirts with a promising message of service on the back. I was the last one to board the plane from our group. As I was stepping onto the aircraft I could hear a middle-aged woman inquire about our shirts to one of our teens. "What group are you and where are you going?"

The teen responded, "Gulfport, Mississippi. We are on a mission trip to serve the people down there." The woman responded graciously and thanked our teen for heading down and serving the poor in the area where people had lost everything in Hurricane Katrina.

This small interaction made me realize there is a world beyond our own that we often ignore, though we still have a relationship with it. The world out there is bigger than you. Bigger than me. Most of the time we block it out or turn it off but it's there. We just need to open ourselves up to our relationship with it, because the world in which we live is a part of who we are.

The real question is how do we find where we lie in this larger than life relationship? People have been looking for an answer to this question for thousands of years. People have turned to philosophy, religion, teachings, or deep meditation. Where is our place in the world? The answer is immeasurably valuable, but it seems to be different for everyone.

What I encourage you to do is to take notice. Take notice of how you interact with other people. How do you treat strangers? Do you open yourself up or close yourself off? When a national or international tragedy takes place, how does it affect you? Are you moved? When a teammate scores the winning goal are you happy for them? When a classmate struggles through a problem but perseveres, do you feel proud?

Take notice of what moves you. Of the people, events, places, and experiences that move you. Take notice. Start growing your relationship from there. Open yourself up to this relationship and it will change you, I promise!

Shoot for the Moon!

It was a sweltering hot day in the Mississippi heat. We were sitting down for lunch in a stifling storage unit full of mattresses that had been donated for people in need. All day, we'd been sweating in the heat, but at the moment, it was gone from our minds. An 82-year-old local volunteer named John had piqued our interest and had all of our ears.

John was an engineer who worked for one of the top aeronautical manufacturers during the infamous "Space Race" to the moon. He spoke in a very articulate way with a matter-of-fact tone. John told us all about the reality of this time in history between the United States and the Soviet Union. I had heard about it in science and history class, but to hear from someone who witnessed it in real life was amazing.

John spoke of the pressure that John F. Kennedy and Lyndon B. Johnson put on NASA and engineers like himself after they made a big promise that the United States would be the first to send people to the moon. At the time, no one knew if it was really possible and how they would go about doing it. People committed themselves to make it work. After all, the president had promised it and there was no way the U.S. was going to let the Russians get there first.

A rocket had to be built. Switches needed to be designed. Astronauts had to be trained. Launchpads had to withstand an incredible blast of power. Weight, energy, gravity (or lack there-of) all had to be taken into account.

It was pretty special to hear John telling this story almost 50 years after Neil Armstrong, Buzz Aldrin, and Michael Collins landed on the moon. John was indeed a part of the rocket that lifted them into space, which was named the *Saturn V*. In part due to John's efforts, the three men made it safely to the moon and back.

While his life story was truly impressive, I was more impressed by John himself. He had lived an exciting life thus far, and no one would have thought differently of him if he stayed at home on his couch, and read the newspaper while sipping some iced tea, enjoying his well-earned retirement.

But that wasn't John. John was here to give. He was giving everything he had. John had a notepad full of people in need of furniture, things to be fixed, and donations he had to pick up. The list was endless. John woke up every day, came to a makeshift office and found a way to help the next person on his list. He worked alongside our teens with the same amount of energy they had. He spoke so highly of everyone he encountered in his life. You could tell he'd had a rich marriage and raised an incredible family.

I told you to take notice and open yourselves up to relationships. I took notice of John. In fact, we all took notice of John. He changed us and he certainly changed me.

When I went to Mississippi and met John I had already written the first draft of this book. As a first time author, you doubt yourself. I was asking myself, *Do teens really need to hear my message? Should I even publish my book?* Then came John.

John's life has not been an easy one, and yet he was one of the most fulfilled and inspiring people I have ever met. I analyzed everything he valued. I want more people to have such fulfilling lives as John. What it came down to was this: John was a master at conversations, relationships, and service. Sound familiar?

PART 3 RECAP:
CRUSHING RELATIONSHIPS

Relationships are the vehicles that help us to live fulfilling and rewarding lives. But even though they serve us, they can also be challenging. Whenever you find yourself stressed by the people in your life, turn to the CPR of Relationships.

1. **C**ommunication
   - Confidence = trust. Can't have a positive relationship without trust.
   - Clear expectations

2. **P**roblem Solve
   - Prepare
   - Past Experiences

3. **R**espect
   - Self-respect is the key
   - Give and receive it

CONCLUSION

As we wrap up our journey, I'd like to take the time to thank you. You have changed my life in more ways than you'll ever know. By buying this book you helped to feed a hungry orphan. You never know how far your impact will reach!

I want to acknowledge how difficult being a teen can be. We have taken on the gargantuan tasks of navigating difficult conversations, traversing the ins and outs of relationships, and putting a pulse on our purpose. Hopefully you have taken away at least one thing that has helped make your life a little bit easier. If this book has impacted you in some way, please let me know and write an honest review on Amazon. This helps you and me to have an even bigger impact on more teens and more orphans!

I am going to leave you with this final note:

You are an incredible person. I wish I could begin to describe how much your life and the story you tell yourself matters. Be curious. Be present. Listen. Find that trusted adult. Master communication. Respect yourself and everyone else. When you get lost, come back to the part of the book where you feel you need some help or just a quick reset. Let the real you shine through. You are going to do incredible things! Now with your hearts blazing, go set the world on fire! You can do it!

Can You Help?

Thank You For Reading My Book!

I really appreciate all of your feedback, and
I love hearing what you have to say.

I need your input to make the next version of
this book and my future books better.

Please leave me an honest review on Amazon letting
me know what you thought of the book.

Thanks so much!

Patrick

ABOUT THE AUTHOR

Patrick has worked with thousands of teens as a teacher, coach, school administrator and youth group leader. He painfully struggled in his teenage years and has committed his life's work to helping teens have happy and healthy lives. Patrick is well-known in the education field and has been named Coach of the Year by the Boston Globe for his work with student-athletes.